# A PASSION FOR COLOR

# A PASSION FOR COLOR

## SARAH BURNETT

### Fashion Photography by ANTHONY CRICKMAY

Macmillan Publishing Company
*New York*

Maxwell Macmillan International
*New York Oxford Singapore Sydney*

Macmillan Publishing Company
866 Third Avenue, New York, NY 10022

Collier Macmillan Canada, Inc.
1200 Eglintorr Avenue East, Suite 200
Don Mills, Ontario M3C 3N1

First published in Great Britain by
Conran Octopus Limited,
37 Shelton Street, London WC2H 9HN

Library of Congress Cataloging-in-Publication Data
Burnett, Sarah.
   A passion for color/by Sarah Burnett:
   photographs by Anthony Crickmay:
   Conran Octopus Limited.
      p. cm.

   ISBN 0-02-518625-6
   1. Knitting–Patterns.  2. Dyes and dyeing, Domestic.
   3. Sweaters.  4. Coats.  I. Crickmay, Anthony.  II. Conran
   Octopus Limited.  III. Title.
   TT825.B86   1990
   746.9'2–dc20                        90–31108

Macmillan books are available at special discounts for bulk
purchases for sales promotions, premiums, fund-raising, or
educational use.
For details, contact:
Special Sales Director
Macmillan Publishing Company
866 Third Avenue
New York, NY 10022

10 9 8 7 6 5 4 3 2 1

Printed in Singapore

# CONTENTS

## INTRODUCTION

8

## COOKING WITH COLOR

## THE PATTERNS

## GLOSSARY

## SUPPLIERS

158

## ACKNOWLEDGMENTS

159

# INTRODUCTION

Colorful clothes have always been my passion. As a teenager I dressed like a rainbow and my wardrobe remains a muddle of different textiles in every imaginable color. Fabrics collected when traveling, or that I have bought or been given, fill every room in the house: Guatemalan weavings, quilted bedspreads, Turkish kilims, hand-rolled felt, and embroidered silks and velvets. Even my old clothes have been given a new lease on life; the crêpe dresses I once eagerly hunted at rummage sales have ended their days as patchwork curtains, the leftovers from the curtains are now a multicolored woven rag rug.

Travel and marriage and moving to the Dorset countryside changed my life considerably. Our small cottage looked out over water meadows. I bought a potter's wheel and kiln and struggled in vain to make brightly colored decorated pots. Our way of life was a classic period piece: my husband wrote novels, we kept sheep and chickens, grew vegetables, baked our own bread and made enough elderflower wine to entertain friends and last out the year.

The arrival of children meant making them winter sweaters. But the gaudy chemical colors of those first sweaters and hats made me long for something softer. I can no longer remember the first time I lowered a hank of wool into a saucepan of plant dye, but the results were a revelation. Outside, in the surrounding woods and meadows, lay the very colors I had been failing to find in my pottery. There was no holding back. Saucepans heaped with wool and enveloped in steam took over the kitchen and transformed the riches of the hedgerow into colors I had only seen in my dreams.

The more I experimented the more I was amazed by the depth and beauty of natural color. Every other plant I gathered seemed capable of producing a new shade. But there were the inevitable disappointments, and I soon discovered that many plants gave muddy yellows, sludge browns, and dirty greens. I planted a dye garden, hoping it would provide the bright blues and reds I was still searching for. For two years I waged war with the weeds, before finally accepting that the temperate English climate just wasn't capable of yielding the strong bright colors I wanted. Some of the best dye plants need sun and heat and it wasn't until I started using dyestuffs imported from South America and Africa that I knew I had found the answer.

Natural dyeing is thousands of years old, whereas chemical dyeing only dates to 1856 when William Perkin, an eighteen-year-old chemistry research assistant, accidentally discovered that an aniline dye could be produced from coal tar. He christened it "mauve" and in 1857, with the help of his father and brother, set up a company in North London to manufacture the mauve dye. The chemical dye industry had been born.

Today, more than a century later, fabrics that don't run or fade come in every conceivable color. Some are so garish that you can almost smell the chemicals that created them. In my opinion, the modern synthetic dye works make little attempt to achieve the endlessly subtle shades possible with natural dyes. You only have to look at an Elizabethan costume or a Baluchi rug to be aware of the gulf that divides plant from chemical dyes.

Natural dyes are not entirely without faults. Some of the colors fade a little and the nature of plants makes it difficult to dye the same shade consistently. But the quality of natural colors is unsurpassed and all the recipes I have included give magnificent colors that mellow and mature. The skill lies in turning their defects into virtues; two

*left* Heaps of knitted sweaters, hanks of yarn, and wool wound into balls and stacked on shelves always fill the workshop with a mass of glorious pattern and vibrant color.

*overleaf* Some of the most picturesque countryside in England lies in Dorset in the South West. Soft rolling hills grazed by sheep or showing the signs of ancient habitation by Iron-Age people lead down to the coast, which can be by turns idyllically peaceful or racked by violent storms.

sweaters may share a pattern, even the same colors, but the variation in the dyeing gives each its uniqueness.

From the start I was determined to combine strong bright colors with extravagant designs and patterns. Just because a sweater is knitted from naturally dyed wool doesn't mean it has to be dull and lifeless. I also wanted my designs to be exciting to wear, even theatrical.

Many years ago I bought some Diaghilev ballet costumes at an auction. Serge Diaghilev was a Russian impresario whose introduction to the West of the Ballets Russes in 1909 transformed ballet and sparked off a revolution in fashion and design. Under him, dancers like Nijinsky and Pavlova danced to the music of Stravinsky wearing costumes designed by Bakst, Picasso, Matisse, and Braque. The braided skirts and wool jackets with their dramatic full Russian sleeves that I bought that day were irresistible. I wore them constantly, and the sleeves of many of my own designs are a small tribute to their influence.

Many ideas have helped to shape my designs, but the knitting technique I use comes from a tiny windswept island in the North Atlantic on the same latitude as Greenland. Fair Isle is one of the most isolated of the Shetland Islands, but its impact on knitting has been immense and not just for the distinctive all-over pattern traditionally associated with it. Over the centuries the islanders have evolved a method by which when one color is in use the others are neatly woven into the back of the knitting. The result is as sturdy as the islanders themselves, with the strength and texture of cloth.

Originally the islanders used plant dyes, a tradition born out of necessity that sadly did not survive the arrival of synthetics. The marriage between natural dyes and Fair Isle techniques is a delight. Multitudes of different colors can be used. The body part of the sweaters is knitted in one piece and the sleeves are grafted on afterward. There are no loose ends to unravel and the inside of the knitting is as perfect as the outside. The extra strength means the sweaters retain their shape and never deteriorate and the technique allows you to mingle in as many colors as you like, though without ever using more than three colors in a row.

The designs I have chosen for the book are the result of many years of experimentation. I am helped by being surrounded by a wonderfully cheerful team of knitters. We work closely together, improving and perfecting ideas, and they are the first to let me know if a design won't work.

I am often asked what inspired a particular design and I have tried to write a bit about each of the ones I have chosen for the book. Yet it hasn't always been easy. Some ideas stem from the colors obtained during the dyeing, but they might just as easily be sparked off by a flower or a scrap of color and pattern in a painting.

What I have tried to do is create contemporary designs that are dramatic and easy to wear, but which still retain classical elegance and style. The combining of two traditional crafts makes the possibilities limitless. The dyeing is like cooking, and is surprisingly easy once a few basics are mastered. Natural dyes make everything you knit an individual creation that might one day become a family heirloom. It is also fun, and once you've made a start there will be no stopping!

*The Fair-Isle technique of weaving colors not in use into the back of the knitting means that garments knitted this way are as neat, and almost as beautiful, on the inside as on the outside.*

# COOKING WITH
# COLOR

# GETTING STARTED

When I first started dyeing I used the plants growing round me in the English countryside. In this I was merely carrying on a tradition begun by primitive man, for natural dyeing is one of the earliest of all crafts. Dyes from shellfish, insects, and plants were used for body decoration before the first textiles were woven, and the earliest fragments of weaving to survive still retain some of their original color.

The Chinese dyed silk with indigo more than 5,000 years ago, and by 1,000 BC the ancient Phoenicians had perfected skills that changed little until the 19th century. It was they who first lowered themselves over cliffs to harvest a lichen called orchil which turned crimson and purple when steeped in stale urine.

By the Middle Ages, weld and dyer's broom were providing cloth mills with Lincoln green and Robin Hood and his men with clothing to match the color of their forest refuge. Dyes that "neither rain, wine, nor yet vinegar can stain" were in common use, and imported plants such as madder and indigo made fortunes for the merchants who traded in them.

My own attempts at gathering natural dyes were more modest. I grew woad (*Isatis tinctoria*) from seed, but otherwise made use of what was seasonally available, or could be dried and stored. Nettles gave dull greens. Elderberry dyes weren't fast – the wool lost color in sunlight. But walnut husks, weld, onion skins, and safflower all proved their worth and I still use them today.

Much of the pleasure came from experimenting with different plants and mordants – the metallic salts used to fix the color. I soon learned that the exact repetition of a precise color was virtually impossible. Plants are dependent on their individual habitats, and weld grown on chalk gave a slightly richer yellow than that grown on clay. Annual variations in climate also had an effect, as did different conditions of storage and drying.

The dye recipes given in this book all employ readily obtainable dyestuffs, some of them imported and available from dye suppliers, and others, such as onion skins, available in or around the home (see page 20). The wool used for dyeing must be unbleached – bleached wools resist dyes. All the patterns in this book have been designed for knitting in unplied Cheviot wool which has very little nap. The Magician's and Adult Fair Isle sweaters have been knitted using two strands of wool. See page 158 for Suppliers and alternative wools.

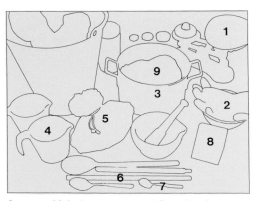

## EQUIPMENT FOR MORDANTING AND DYEING

1 Weighing scales
2 Rubber gloves
3 One-gallon stainless steel saucepan, used for mordanting and dyeing only
4 One 2-cup heatproof glass measuring cup
5 Muslin or nylon bag for tying up dyestuffs
6 Stick for stirring
7 Teaspoon
8 Olive oil soap (or other natural soap)
9 4-ounce hanks of wool

See page 30 for key to equipment for indigo dyeing.

# MORDANTING

Mordanting always precedes dyeing. It is the method by which a mordant – one of a range of metallic salts – is used to make the color fast. Without it natural dyeing would be impossible and, apart from indigo dyeing, which is a process unlike any other, there is only one dye recipe in this book that doesn't require a mordant. Different mordants give different colors from the same dyestuff; thus, by varying the mordant, cochineal can produce either red, pink, or purple.

The process is very simple and certainly more scientific than in the past, when such things as wood ash, copper filings, and bran were used. One tale even tells of a dead cat being thrown into a vat by a dyer desperate to get the color he wanted!

## MORDANTS

All mordants must be clearly labeled "poisonous" and stored in a safe dry place out of reach of children. Take them out only when you are ready to use them and put them away again as soon as you have measured out what you need. See Suppliers (page 158) for names and addresses of suppliers of mordants.

### ALUM
potassium aluminium sulfate
This is traditionally the most important of all the ancient mordants and was used with madder as early as 2,000 BC. Using too much alum makes the wool sticky. Alum is now supplied as a white powder.

### COPPER SULFATE
This is often known as "blue copperas" and is the most common of the copper mordants. The blue crystals are poisonous and should always be handled with particular care.

### CHROME
potassium dichromate, bichromate of potash
This metal was introduced in about 1800 and is widely used with red dyes. The orange crystals are sensitive to light: store them in a dark place.

### TIN
stannous chloride
Tin is always used in very small quantities and should be rinsed out thoroughly after mordanting as it makes wool brittle, but it is superb for brightening reds. It is supplied as white crystals.

### OXALIC ACID
This is corrosive and so needs to be handled with special care – always wear gloves. Natural oxalic acid is found in garden sorrel and rhubarb stalks. It is supplied commercially as a white powder.

### ACETIC ACID
vinegar
This is used in small quantities to help the wool absorb the mordant.

### CREAM OF TARTAR
tartaric acid
This helps to soften the wool when harsh mordants are used. It is supplied as a white powder and is also used in baking.

## MORDANTING METHOD

The method is the same for all the mordants used in this book. Follow the recipes given on pages 24–28 for quantities.

1 Tie a 4-ounce hank of unbleached wool in a loose figure of eight. Tie it in four places to stop tangling.

2 Wash and wet the wool thoroughly.

3 Measure the mordant into the heatproof glass measuring cup. Add ½ cup of warm water and stir until dissolved.

4 Put 8 cups of warm water into the saucepan, place on medium heat, and add the mordant mixture. Stir.

5 Put the wet wool into the saucepan and stir. Simmer gently for 30 minutes.

6 Remove the wool and throw away the water in the saucepan. Wash out the saucepan to ready it for dyeing.

7 Gently squeeze the excess water from the wool and then keep it wet (in a plastic bag if necessary), ready for dyeing.

# NATURAL DYESTUFFS

The dyestuffs listed on this page are all available from dye suppliers or found in the home. But all plants or berries which stain can probably be employed in natural dyeing, and you can be sure of results by using those which include the Latin name *tinctoria*, meaning "to stain." Leave all rare flowers alone, but otherwise don't be afraid of experimenting with common local plants. Simply pick twice the weight of plantstuff to that of the wool you want to dye, having first mordanted the wool with an alum mordant (see pages 18–19). Boil the plant in twice its volume of water until the water changes color, add the wool and simmer until the wool has colored. Wash the wool and dry it. Try to record the plants used, the time of year they were picked, and keep samples of the dyed wool for reference.

## 1 BRAZILWOOD
### *Caesalpinia braziliensis*
Described in the 18th century as giving the color of claret wine, these dark wood chippings dye a range of reds, browns, and burgundies. The dye is at its most concentrated in the heartwood. Other trees in the family include peachwood and **REDWOOD**. Before the discovery of the Americas most brazilwood came from India, but so much was found growing in part of South America that it gave its name to a country – Brazil.

## 2 COCHINEAL
### *Coccus cacti*

> Painted for sight and essenced for the smell
> Like a frigate fraught with spice and cochineal,
> Sail in the ladies.

So wrote Alexander Pope, noting cochineal's role as a color dye in cosmetics. It is obtained from a dried insect that lives on the prickly pear cactus and provides the most brilliant reds and pinks, including Huntsman's scarlet. The cacti are grown as a crop in Central America, the West Indies, and the Canary Islands, and the insects are brushed off at harvest time.

## 3 FUSTIC
### *Chlorophora tinctoria*
These yellow chippings come from the dyer's mulberry tree, or Cuba fustic, which grows in the West Indies and Mexico. The dye it produces is extremely fast and, combined with other plants, it was used to dye khaki before the invention of a suitable synthetic. I get vibrant yellows and golds, and a glorious green when 'top dyed' with indigo.

## 4 INDIGO
### *Indigofera tinctoria*
Historically the most famous of all dyes, this blue powder is extracted from the leaves of *Indigofera*, a plant genus grown widely throughout the tropics. The leaves are fermented, and the sediment dried and ground to prepare it for dyeing. Its blues are outstanding, and it is still widely used in India. The analysis of natural indigo followed by its synthetic manufacture in 1897 led directly to the evolution of blue denim.

## 5 LOGWOOD
### *Haemotoxylon campechianum*
I use logwood chips for deep navy blues and soft grays. The trees grow widely in Mexico and the Caribbean, where the yellow timber turns brown as soon as it is felled. It is another dye of historical importance, mainly because there was no equivalent in the Old World and it is the only plant dye to give a true black on wool.

## 6 MADDER
### *Rubia tinctorum*
This is a dye renowned for its reds and extracted from the root of a herbaceous plant which grows widely throughout Europe and the Middle East, especially France and Turkey. The medieval papal court owed the scarlet robes of its cardinals to madder, but there are fragments dyed with it which date back to at least 3,000 BC. Old roots have the richest concentration of color, and the plant grows best on chalk. It can be grown domestically but the root is also commercially supplied chopped and I use it for a range of beautiful dusty pinks.

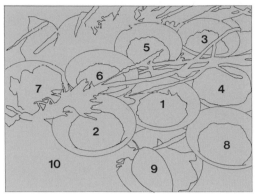

## 7 ONIONS

*Allium cepa*

Yellow onion skins are undoubtedly the most common and easiest of all dyestuffs, and they give me wonderful rusts and pale browns. Just peel off the outer dry skin whenever you need an onion for cooking and store the skins in a paper bag until needed. Red onion skins will give a diffcrent shade of yellow.

## 8 WALNUT HUSKS/9 LEAVES

*Juglans regia, Juglans nigra*

This is the only dye I don't combine with a mordant, although when mordanted with alum the dried leaves do give various shades of brown. It is a "substantive" dye which does not require a mordant to make it fast. I collect the fallen shells and husks from the tree, storing them in a jar of water in a dark cupboard until needed. However, they are supplied as chopped chips, so don't despair if a tree doesn't grow nearby.

## 10 WELD

*Reseda luteola*

This tall elegant biennial plant is my favourite dye plant, and is easily grown. It is also known as wild mignonette or dyer's rocket, and for centuries its bright yellows have been used for dyeing. There is little variation in results between the fresh and the dried plant, but hang it upside down in bundles if you want to store it.

See Suppliers (page 158) for suppliers of natural dyestuffs.

# DYEING

Before you start dyeing there are a few points to bear in mind. Do not expect the wool to be an even color when dyed; it may be patchy – mine always is – this is part of the charm of naturally dyed wool. Moreover, all dyestuffs will give a slightly different color each time they are used. Natural dyes are not uniform. Experiment a little with the dyes – use these recipes as foundations on which to build.

Be careful when using dyestuffs. Always wear rubber gloves and keep children out of the way where possible. The dyestuffs are no more poisonous than ordinary household cleaners but exercise the same amount of care with their storage and use. Always wash the wool carefully to stop it from tangling and felting.

Enjoy using natural dyes and have fun. Don't worry if you get entirely the wrong color. Use your imagination and change the colors intended for the design: it always works. I try to design all of my sweaters to make the best use of naturally dyed colors; thus colors which would clash if chemically dyed merge and mix as a harmonious whole. The colors may be bright, but they are never gaudy.

## METHOD FOR DYEING

This method of dyeing applies to all the recipes in this book except for indigo (see pages 30–31). However, there are slight variations so follow the specific instructions for individual colors on the following pages.

1 Put 8 cups of water into the stainless steel saucepan.

2 Add the dyestuff according to the recipe. Stir.

3 Put the mordanted wool (see pages 18–19) into the saucepan and simmer for the length of time given in the recipe. Do not stir the wool; turn it over once.

4 Remove the pan from the heat and allow the wool to cool in the pan.

5 Remove the dyed wool and wash well with warm water and olive oil soap or other natural soap. Handle the wool very gently to avoid tangling and felting.

6 Rinse the wool until the water runs clear.

7 Hang the wool out on a washing line to dry.

*centre left* Finely ground cochineal, logwood chips tied in a muslin bag, and onion skins have been added to pans of water (step *2*). *main picture left* Simmering in the dyes (step *3*) transforms natural-colored wool into brilliant shades of crimson, navy, and buttercup yellow. *above* After the wool has been dyed it is washed with warm water and soap and then thoroughly rinsed (step *6*).

# REDS

### CRIMSON

**Mordant**  1 teaspoon cream of tartar
        ½ teaspoon tin
**Dyestuff**  1 ounce cochineal, finely ground
**Wool**  4-ounce hank of natural yarn

See pages 18–19 for mordanting instructions.

Mix the cochineal to a smooth paste with a little warm water in a stainless steel saucepan. Add 8 cups of cold water to the paste. Stir well.

Put the mordanted wool into the saucepan and place over a very low heat. Bring to the boil very slowly and gently simmer for 20 minutes. Remove from the heat and allow the wool to cool in the pan.

Remove the dyed wool and wash well with warm water and olive oil soap or other natural soap. Rinse the wool until the water runs clear, then hang out, to dry.

### SCARLET

**Mordant**  ½ teaspoon oxalic acid
        ½ teaspoon tin
        1 teaspoon cream of tartar
**Dyestuff**  1 ounce cochineal, finely ground
**Wool**  4-ounce hank of natural yarn

Method as for Crimson

### RED

**Mordant**  1 ounce alum
**Dyestuff**  6 ounces brazilwood, tied in a muslin bag
**Wool**  4-ounce hank of natural yarn

See pages 18–19 for mordanting instructions.

Put the bag of brazilwood into a stainless steel saucepan with 10 cups of water and boil for 1 hour. Remove the bag of brazilwood.

Put the mordanted wool into the saucepan and simmer for 30 minutes. Remove from the heat and allow the wool to cool in the pan.

Remove the dyed wool and wash well with warm water and olive oil soap or other natural soap. Rinse the wool until the water runs clear, then hang out to dry.

1  crimson
2  scarlet
3  red

# PINKS

### MAGENTA

**Mordant**  1 ounce alum
**Dyestuff**  1 ounce cochineal, finely ground
**Wool**  4-ounce hank of natural yarn

See pages 18–19 for mordanting instructions.

Mix the cochineal to a smooth paste with a little warm water in a stainless steel saucepan. Add 8 cups of cold water to the paste. Stir well.

Put the mordanted wool into the saucepan and place over a very low heat. Bring to the boil very slowly and gently simmer for 20 minutes. Remove from the heat and allow the wool to cool in the pan.

Remove the dyed wool, wash well, rinse, and then hang out to dry.

### PINK

**Mordant**  1 ounce alum
**Dyestuff**  1 teaspoon cochineal, finely ground
**Wool**  4-ounce hank of natural yarn

Method as for Magenta

### PALE PINK

**Mordant**  1 ounce alum
**Dyestuff**  ½ teaspoon cochineal, finely ground
**Wool**  4-ounce hank of natural yarn

Method as for Magenta

### REDWOOD PINK

**Mordant**  1 ounce alum
**Dyestuff**  3 ounces redwood, tied in a muslin bag
**Wool**  4-ounce hank of natural yarn

See pages 18–19 for mordanting instructions.

Put the bag of redwood into a stainless steel saucepan with 10 cups of water and boil for 1 hour. Remove the bag of redwood.

Put the mordanted wool into the saucepan and simmer for 30 minutes. Remove from the heat and allow the wool to cool in the pan.

Remove the dyed wool, wash well, rinse, and then hang out to dry.

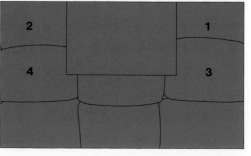

1  magenta
2  pink
3  pale pink
4  redwood pink

# WINES

### ELDERBERRY

**Mordant**  ½ teaspoon chrome
**Dyestuff**  3 ounces brazilwood, tied in a muslin bag
**Wool**  4-ounce hank of natural yarn

See pages 18–19 for mordanting instructions.
    Put the bag of brazilwood into a stainless steel saucepan with 10 cups of water and boil for 1 hour. Remove the dyestuff.
    Put the mordanted wool into the saucepan and simmer for 30 minutes. Remove from the heat and allow the wool to cool in the pan.
    Remove the dyed wool, wash well, rinse, and then hang out to dry.

### LIGHT ELDERBERRY

**Mordant**  ½ teaspoon chrome
**Dyestuff**  1 ounce brazilwood, tied in a muslin bag
**Wool**  4-ounce hank of natural yarn

Method as for Elderberry

### GRAPE

**Mordant**  ½ teaspoon chrome
**Dyestuff**  1 ounce cochineal, finely ground
**Wool**  4-ounce hank of natural yarn

Method as for Crimson

### BURGUNDY

**Mordant**  ½ teaspoon copper sulfate
         ½ teaspoon acetic acid
**Dyestuff**  6 ounces brazilwood, tied in a muslin bag
**Wool**  4-ounce hank of natural yarn

Method as for Elderberry

### MADDER

**Mordant**  ½ teaspoon chrome
**Dyestuff**  4 ounces madder chips, tied in a muslin bag
**Wool**  4-ounce hank of natural yarn

See pages 18–19 for mordanting instructions.
    Put the bag of madder chips into a stainless steel saucepan with 10 cups of cold water. Stir well.
    Put the mordanted wool into the saucepan. Bring to simmering point very slowly and gently simmer for 20 minutes. Do not boil. Remove from the heat and allow to cool in the pan.
    Remove the dyed wool, wash well, rinse, and then hang out to dry.

# NAVY AND GRAYS

### NAVY

**Mordant**  ½ teaspoon copper sulfate
**Dyestuff**  2 ounces logwood, tied in a muslin bag
**Wool**  4-ounce hank of natural yarn

See pages 18–19 for mordanting instructions.
    Put the bag of logwood into a stainless steel saucepan with 10 cups of water and boil for 45 minutes. Remove the bag of logwood.
    Put the mordanted wool into the saucepan and simmer for 20 minutes. Remove from the heat and allow to cool in the pan.
    Remove the dyed wool and then wash well with warm water and olive oil soap or other natural soap. Rinse the wool until the water runs clear, then hang out to dry.

### DARK GRAY

**Mordant**  ½ teaspoon chrome
**Dyestuff**  ½ ounce logwood, tied in a muslin bag
**Wool**  4-ounce hank of natural yarn

Method as for Navy

### GRAY

**Mordant**  ½ teaspoon chrome
**Dyestuff**  1 teaspoon logwood
**Wool**  4-ounce hank of natural yarn

Method as for Navy

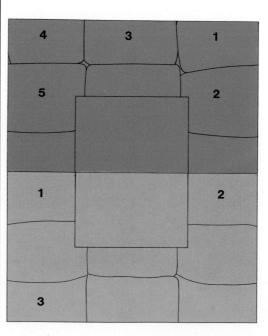

1  elderberry
2  light elderberry
3  grape
4  burgundy
5  madder

1  navy
2  dark gray
3  gray

## YELLOWS

### BUTTERCUP YELLOW

**Mordant**  1 ounce alum
**Dyestuff**  1 ounce onion skins
**Wool**  4-ounce hank of natural yarn

See pages 18–19 for mordanting instructions.

Put the onion skins into a stainless steel saucepan with 8 cups of water and simmer for 30 minutes.

Put the mordanted wool into the saucepan and simmer for a good 20 minutes. Remove from the heat and allow the wool to cool in the pan.

Remove the dyed wool and wash well with warm water and olive oil soap or other natural soap. Rinse well, then hang out to dry.

### YELLOW

**Mordant**  1 ounce alum
**Dyestuff**  3 ounces weld, chopped
**Wool**  4-ounce hank of natural yarn

See pages 18–19 for mordanting instructions.

Put the weld into a stainless steel saucepan with 8 cups of water and boil for 30 minutes.

Put the mordanted wool into the saucepan and simmer for a good 20 minutes. Remove from the heat and allow the wool to cool in the pan.

Remove the dyed wool and wash well with warm water and olive oil soap or other natural soap. Rinse well, then hang out to dry.

### PRIMROSE

**Mordant**  1 ounce alum
**Dyestuff**  1 teaspoon fustic chips, tied in a muslin bag
**Wool**  4-ounce hank of natural yarn

See pages 18–19 for mordanting instructions.

Put the bag of fustic into a stainless steel saucepan with 8 cups of water and boil for 40 minutes.

Put the mordanted wool into the saucepan and stir. Simmer for 20 minutes. Remove from the heat and allow the wool to cool in the pan.

Remove the dyed wool and wash well with warm water and olive oil soap or other natural soap. Rinse well, then hang out to dry.

## OCHRE AND WALNUTS

### OCHRE

**Mordant**  ½ teaspoon chrome
**Dyestuff**  1 ounce onion skins
**Wool**  4-ounce hank of natural yarn

See pages 18–19 for mordanting instructions.

Put the onion skins into a stainless steel saucepan with 8 cups of water and simmer for 30 minutes.

Put the mordanted wool into the saucepan and simmer for 30 minutes. Remove from the heat and allow the wool to cool in the pan.

Remove the dyed wool and wash well with warm water and olive oil soap or other natural soap. Rinse the wool, then hang out to dry.

### WALNUT

**Mordant**  1 ounce alum
**Dyestuff**  1 ounce walnut husks
**Wool**  4-ounce hank of natural yarn

See pages 18–19 for mordanting instructions.

Put the walnut husks into a stainless steel saucepan with 8 cups of water and simmer for 40 minutes.

Put the mordanted wool into the saucepan and simmer for 40 minutes. Remove from the heat and allow the wool to cool in the pan.

Remove the dyed wool and wash well with warm water and olive oil soap or other natural soap. Rinse the wool, then hang out to dry.

### PALE WALNUT

**No mordant**
**Dyestuff**  1 ounce walnut leaves
**Wool**  4-ounce hank of natural yarn

Put the walnut leaves into a stainless steel saucepan with 8 cups of water and simmer for 40 minutes.

Wet thoroughly the hank of *unmordanted* wool. Put the wool into the saucepan and simmer for 30 minutes. Remove from the heat and allow the wool to cool in the pan.

Remove the dyed wool and wash well with warm water and olive oil soap or other natural soap. Rinse the wool, then hang out to dry.

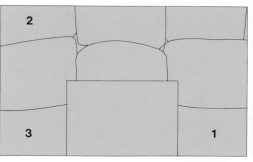

1 buttercup yellow
2 yellow
3 primrose

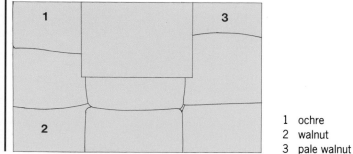

1 ochre
2 walnut
3 pale walnut

# INDIGO DYEING

Indigo dyeing is unlike any other dyeing process. Because the blue powder is not easily soluble in water, a stock solution is prepared. The powder is mixed into a smooth paste with a solution of caustic soda and then the oxygen in the mixture is eliminated by adding a solution of sodium dithionite (see Suppliers, page 158), which turns the paste into a greenish-yellow liquid. The wool is immersed in a dye bath made with the stock solution, and finally oxidizes as it comes out, changing from yellow to blue. The process is quite straightforward. Be very careful as some of the ingredients are toxic and indigo stains easily. Keep the bucket or saucepan for indigo dyeing only.

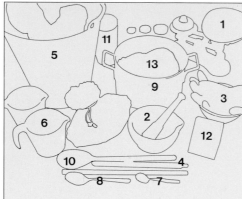

## EQUIPMENT

1   Weighing scales
2   Pestle and mortar
3   Rubber gloves
4   Water thermometer
5   One-gallon stainless steel bucket (or saucepan)
6   Two 2-cup heatproof glass measuring cups
7   Teaspoon
8   Household saucepan
9   Stick for stirring
10  One-quart glass jar
11  Olive oil soap (or other natural soap)
12  4-ounce hanks of wool

## METHOD FOR INDIGO DYEING
### Preparing Indigo Stock Solution

1 ounce natural powdered indigo
1½ ounces caustic soda
1 ounce sodium dithionite

1   Put the indigo powder into a mortar and grind to a smooth creamy paste with a little warm water and a pestle.

2   Measure 1 cup of warm water into a heatproof glass measuring cup and add the caustic soda. Stir until dissolved.

3   Measure 1 cup of warm water into another heatproof glass measuring cup and add the sodium dithionite, stirring *very gently* to dissolve it.

4   Pour the indigo paste into a quart jar. Rinse the pestle with a little more water, holding it over the jar in order not to waste any indigo.

5   Add the caustic soda solution to the jar.

6   Add the solution of sodium dithionite carefully to the jar, trying not to create any air bubbles. Stir very gently.

7   Stand the jar in a pan of very hot water. Keep checking that the temperature of the liquid in the jar does not exceed 140°F. Let this stand for 30 to 60 minutes until the liquid in the jar is a murky yellow-green. The indigo stock solution is now ready for use and can be stored for up to 6 weeks.

## Preparing an Indigo Dye Bath

**8** Fill a special stainless steel bucket or saucepan with 10 cups of warm water.

**9** Sprinkle one teaspoon of sodium dithionite onto the warm water to reduce the oxygen.

**10** Heat the water very gently. The temperature should be somewhere between 120° and 140°F. The water should never exceed 140°F – overheating is disastrous because it will turn the wool brown.

## Completing Indigo Dyeing

**11** Prepare the dye bath as above.

**12** Thoroughly wet the wool.

**13** Measure out the indigo stock solution according to the recipe for the shade of indigo that you require (see over) and add very carefully to the dye bath. Stir extremely gently.

**14** Put on rubber gloves and dip the wetted wool into the bath for the number of seconds specified in the recipe, squeezing it gently under water to make sure that the indigo is absorbed. Lift the wool *gently* out of the bath and watch it turn from yellow to greenish blue in the air.

**15** Dip the wool again according to the recipe and watch the color change when you lift it out.

**16** Hang the wool out on a washing line for 30 minutes to oxidize again.

**17** Wash the wool very thoroughly with warm water and olive oil soap or other natural soap. Rinse it until the water runs clear, then hang it out to dry.

*Greens are created by first dyeing wool yellow then dyeing it for a second time in an indigo dye bath. The wool changes color from yellow to green as it emerges into the air and oxidizes.*

# INDIGO BLUES

### DARK INDIGO BLUE

3 tablespoons Indigo Stock Solution (page 30)
4-ounce hank of natural yarn

Prepare an indigo dye bath (see page 30).

Thoroughly wet the wool. Measure out the stock solution and add very carefully to the dye bath. Stir extremely gently.

Put on rubber gloves and dip the wetted wool into the bath for 60 seconds (count to 60), squeezing it gently under water to make sure that the indigo is absorbed. Lift the wool gently out of the bath and watch it turn from yellow to greenish blue in the air. Dip the wool for another 60 seconds and watch it turn a darker blue when you lift it out again.

Hang the wool out on a washing line for 30 minutes, then wash it very thoroughly with warm water and olive oil soap or other natural soap. Rinse the wool until the water runs clear, then hang it out to dry.

### MEDIUM INDIGO BLUE

4½ teaspoons Indigo Stock Solution (page 30)
4-ounce hank of natural yarn

Prepare the dye bath and follow the method for Dark Indigo Blue, but dip the wool *three* times for only 10 seconds each time.

### PALE INDIGO BLUE

1½ teaspoons Indigo Stock Solution (page 30)
4-ounce hank of natural yarn

Prepare the dye bath and follow the method for Dark Indigo Blue but dip the wool *once* for only 10 seconds.

# GREENS

The most exquisite greens are produced by "top dyeing" wool that has first been dyed yellow in an indigo bath.

### GRASS GREEN

**Ingredients for yellow (page 28)**

| | |
|---|---|
| **Mordant** | 1 ounce alum |
| **Dyestuff** | 3 ounces weld |
| **Top dye** | 4½ teaspoons Indigo Stock Solution (page 30) |
| **Wool** | 4-ounce hank of natural yarn |

See pages 18–19 for mordanting instructions, then follow procedure for Yellow (page 28).

Top dye the wool, following the procedure for Medium Indigo Blue.

### OLIVE GREEN

**Ingredients for Primrose (page 28)**

| | |
|---|---|
| **Mordant** | 1 ounce alum |
| **Dyestuff** | 2 ounces fustic chips, tied in a muslin bag |
| **Top dye** | 4½ teaspoons Indigo Stock Solution (page 30) |
| **Wool** | 4-ounce hank of natural yarn |

See pages 18–19 for mordanting instructions, then follow procedure for Primrose (page 28).

Top dye the wool, following the procedure for Medium Indigo Blue.

### BLUE-GREEN

**Ingredients for yellow (page 28)**

| | |
|---|---|
| **Mordant** | 1 ounce alum |
| **Dyestuff** | 1 ounce weld |
| **Top dye** | 3 tablespoons Indigo Stock Solution (page 30) |
| **Wool** | 4-ounce hank of natural yarn |

See pages 18–19 for mordanting instructions, then follow procedure for Yellow (page 28).

Top dye the wool, following the procedure for Dark Indigo Blue.

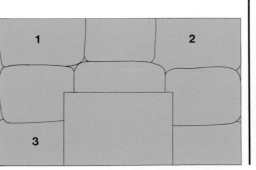

1 dark indigo blue
2 medium indigo blue
3 pale indigo blue

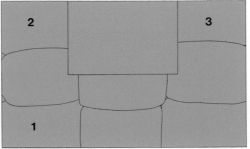

1 grass green
2 olive green
3 blue-green

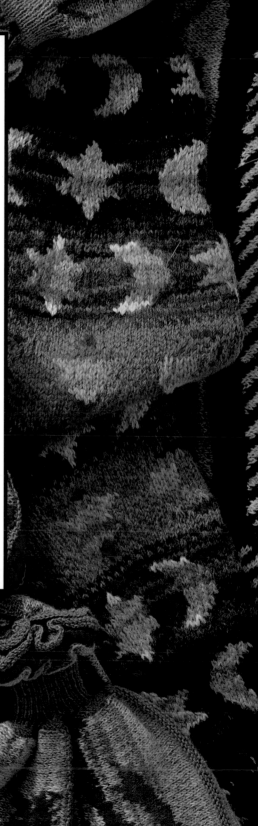

# THE PATTERNS

● The **Glossary of Knitting Terms and Techniques** (page 154) contains tips and information which will help you greatly in knitting the garments, so read it **before** you start to knit.

● All the garments are designed to be knitted in unplied (single ply) Cheviot wool unless otherwise stated. For garments requiring plied wool, you can use two strands of unplied wool twisted together or buy 2 ply wool.

● It is essential to knit a sample square before you start the pattern, changing the needle size if necessary to obtain the gauge required.

● In general, the pattern charts are colored to correspond to the garments in the photographs. However, natural dyeing does not produce a consistent strength of color and the garments are designed to make the most of this varied effect. Where a random effect is intended, the charts are also colored randomly. There are no rigid rules and it is open to you to use the colors in the creative combination of your choice.

● When working from the charts, begin at stitch 1, row 1 unless otherwise stated. Follow the chart, repeating as necessary, to the end of the row. Rows will not always begin and end with a complete pattern repeat, therefore when working subsequent rows be sure to start with the stitch immediately above the last stitch worked on the chart.

● Under the **Materials** listed for each pattern, a pair of needles is usually given for the main part of the knitting. When large numbers of stitches are being worked, you can substitute a long circular needle and work in rows.

● The garments should be washed carefully by hand with a neutral washing agent in lukewarm water. You should always spin the water out of them in a washing machine to prevent them from losing their shape, but do not spin dry.

● Abbreviations used in the patterns:

| | |
|---|---|
| **beg** | beginning |
| **ch st** | chain stitch |
| **cont** | continue |
| **dec** | decrease |
| **d m st** | double moss stitch |
| **inc** | increase |
| **k** | knit |
| **k2 tog** | knit 2 stitches together |
| **m st** | moss stitch |
| **p** | purl |
| **patt** | pattern |
| **rem** | remaining |
| **rep** | repeat |
| **rev St st** | reverse stockinette stitch |
| **sl st** | slip st |
| **St st** | stockinette stitch |
| **tog** | together |

# ADULT FAIR ISLE SWEATER

The first sweaters I knitted using natural dyes were Fair Isle. They were robust, light, and the colors suited the all-over patterning. Mine differ from the traditional design because each time the patterning is repeated the color combinations change. The thicker yarn and tapering sleeves make this one quicker to knit. I have deliberately avoided giving specific instructions as to how the colors should be put together as naturally dyed colors never clash, and it's fun trying different combinations. Simply change colors every time you complete the patterning on the graph.

## MATERIALS
Circular size 2 (2¼ mm) needle 29 in (73.5 cm) long
Set of 4 double-pointed size 2 (2¼ mm) needles
Circular size 6 (4 mm) needles 16 in (40 cm) and 29 in (73.5 cm) long
Pair of size 6 (4 mm) needles
7 stitch holders

## WEIGHT OF YARN AND COLORS
**Plied yarn**
17 colors in 2 oz (57 g) balls
6 oz (170 g) in one color (A) for ribs
(Instead of plied yarn you can use 2 strands of ordinary yarn, knitted together.)

## MEASUREMENTS
Length from top of shoulder to bottom edge of sweater: 30 in (76 cm)
Actual width all around at underarm: 48 in (122 cm)
Sleeve length: 23 in (58.5 cm)

## GAUGE
Over pattern, using size 6 (4 mm) needles (or size to obtain gauge), 23 stitches and 25 rows to 4 in (10 cm).

## IMPORTANT
• The colors you use for this pattern are entirely up to you, so each sweater will be unique. Use as many colors

Top of garment

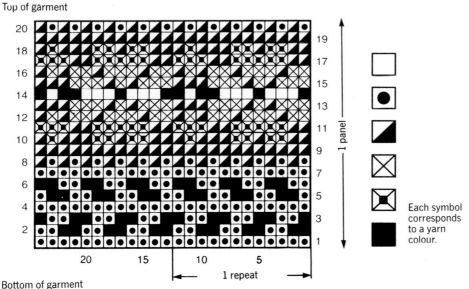

Bottom of garment

Odd-numbered rows are knit, worked from right to left.

Even-numbered rows are purl, worked from left to right.

Each symbol corresponds to a yarn colour.

brightly colored wool around the first stitch each time you begin a round so that you can find the beginning.

● The sleeves are knitted on a circular needle and worked from shoulder to cuff, so remember to reverse the order of the pattern; that is, you work from row 20 to row 1.

## INSTRUCTIONS
### FRONT AND BACK

With size 2 (2¼ mm) circular needle and A, cast on 240 sts. Join.

Work 24 rounds in k1 p1 rib.

**Inc round** *k4, inc into next st: rep from * around (288 sts).

Change to size 6 (4 mm) 29 in (73.5 cm) long circular needle and work rounds 1–20 of chart 5 times (100 rounds).

### Divide for front and back

Slip 1st 14 sts onto a st holder (holder 1) for underarm then patt 116 sts for back. Leave rem sts on circular needle and, with pair of size 6 (4 mm) needles, work straight on these 116 sts until 3 complete panels and 1 row have been worked.

**Row 2** With wrong side facing patt 39 sts, turn.

**Row 3** k2 tog, patt to end.

**Row 4** patt 38 sts, turn.

**Row 5** k2 tog, patt to end (37 sts).

**Rows 6 and 7** as chart, then slip these 37 sts onto a st holder for left back shoulder. With wrong side facing, slip next 38 sts onto a st holder for back neck. Cont on rem 39 sts as follows:

**Row 2** With wrong side facing patt to end.

**Row 3** patt to last 2 sts, k2 tog, turn.

**Row 4** patt, turn.

**Row 5** patt to last 2 sts, k2 tog, turn (37 sts).

**Rows 6 and 7** as chart, then slip these 37 sts onto a st holder for right back shoulder. With right side facing, slip next 28 sts onto a st holder for left underarm (holder 2). Patt 116 sts and slip rem 14 sts onto holder 1. With size 6 (4 mm) needles, work 2 complete panels and 4 rows on these 116 sts for front.

**Row 5** patt 43 sts, turn.

**Row 6** bind off 2 sts, patt to end.

**Row 7** as chart.

**Row 8** bind off 2 sts, patt to end.

**Row 9** as chart.

**Row 10** bind off 1 st, patt to end.

**Row 11** as chart.

**Row 12** bind off 1 st, patt to end (37 sts).

Work straight until row 7 of next panel has been worked, then slip sts onto a st holder for left front shoulder. Slip next 30 sts onto a st holder for front neck and then work rem 43 sts (right side facing) as follows:

**Row 5** bind off 2 sts, patt to end.

**Row 6** as chart.

**Row 7** bind off 2 sts, patt to end.

**Row 8** as chart.

**Row 9** bind off 1 st, patt to end.

as you wish but make sure that every panel has a different color sequence.

● When working front and back the "dots" on row 20 of the panel should be worked in the same color as the "dots" on rows 1–8 of following pattern, as they are part of same color stripe.

● When working St st using just one color, twist a spare ball of the same color yarn across the back of

work to keep the thickness of the garment even.

● The sweater is knitted on a circular needle as far as the underarm, so every round of the chart up to that point is knit.

● When using the circular needles, take great care on the first round to ensure that the stitches are not twisted around the needle.

● When knitting in the round, loop a short strand of

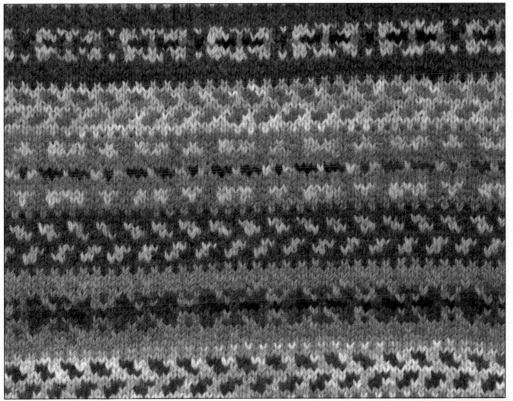

**Row 10** as chart.
**Row 11** bind off 1 st, patt to end (37 sts).
Work straight until work matches left side of neck. Leave sts on a spare needle for right front shoulder.

### Shoulder seams

Block (see page 155) garment and press carefully on wrong side using a damp cloth. With right sides tog graft (see page 155) right front shoulder to right back shoulder and left front shoulder to left back shoulder. Weave in any loose ends using a darning needle (do not just cut them off).

### SLEEVES

Remember to k all rounds and panels in rev order – from round 20–1.
With right side facing and size 6 (4 mm) 16 in (40 cm) long circular needle, slip last 14 sts from holder 1 onto left needle and k them using 1st color you used for 6th panel of front and back. Then pick up and k 58 sts up to shoulder seam, 58 sts down to st holder and then k the 14 sts left on holder (144 sts). Then, using 1st 2 colors you used for 6th panel of front and back, work chart in rev order, rounds 8–2.
**Round 1** *k10, k2 tog; rep from * around (132 sts).
**Rounds 20–2** use same colors as 5th panel of front and back.
**Round 1** *k9, k2 tog; rep from * around (120 sts).
**Rounds 20–2** use same colors as 4th panel of front and back.
**Round 1** *k8, k2 tog; rep from * around (108 sts).
**Rounds 20–2** use same colors as 3rd panel of front and back.
**Round 1** *k7, k2 tog; rep from * around (96 sts).
**Rounds 20–2** use same colors as 2nd panel of front and back.
**Round 1** *k6, k2 tog; rep from * around (84 sts).
**Rounds 20–1** use same colors as 1st panel of front and back, then change to set of 4 double-pointed size 2 (2¼ mm) needles and join on A.
**Next round** *k2 tog, k2; rep from * to last 4 sts, k2 tog, k2 tog (62 sts). Then work 30 rounds in k1 p1 rib. Bind off loosely in rib.

### NECKBAND

With right side facing and size 2 (2¼ mm) double-pointed needles and A, k the 38 sts for back of neck, pick up and k 27 sts along left side of neck, k the 30 sts for front of neck and pick up and k 27 sts along right side of neck (122 sts). Join. Work 9 rounds in k1 p1 rib.
**Next round** p (to make foldline). Work 9 more rounds in k1 p1 rib, then bind off loosely in rib. Fold band to inside along foldline and stitch down neatly.

### FINISHING

Weave in any loose ends using a darning needle (do not just cut them off). Block (see page 155) garment and press carefully using a damp cloth, but do not press ribbing.

# CHILD'S FAIR ISLE CARDIGAN

Cardigans like this one were the first I ever made for my children when they were small. Baking bread, growing vegetables, keeping chickens and sheep, and dyeing wool and knitting were all part of the cottage economy we practiced. I designed them with large Russian sleeves and tight cuffs so that they wouldn't be outgrown too quickly and so that the elbows wouldn't wear out. The generous shape meant that the cardigan would fit a two year old (admittedly almost down to the knees) as easily as a six or seven year old. I always knitted them in as many colors as possible, changing the colors after each set of patterning. Because they are small, the dyeing and knitting are not too daunting. Children love wearing them, and one I knitted many years ago has already been passed down from one generation to the next as if it were a family heirloom.

### MATERIALS

Pair of size 2 (2¼ mm) needles
Set of 4 double-pointed size 2 (2¼ mm) needles
Pair of size 3 (3¼ mm) needles
Circular size 3 (3¼ mm) needle 16 in (40 cm) long
6 stitch holders
6 buttons

### WEIGHT OF YARN AND COLORS

14 oz (400 g) in as many colors as required

### MEASUREMENTS

Length from top of shoulder to bottom edge of cardigan: 18 in (46 cm)
Actual width all around at underarm: 30 in (76 cm)
Sleeve length: 13½ in (34 cm)

### GAUGE

Over pattern, using size 3 (3¼ mm) needles (or size to obtain gauge), 31 stitches and 32 rows to 4 in (10 cm).

### IMPORTANT

● The choice of colorway is entirely up to you but every panel must have a different sequence of colors. This means that each cardigan will be unique.
● Twist wools at back of work every 1–2 sts to avoid making holes, but do not pull tight.
● When working St st using just one color, twist a spare ball of the same color yarn across the back of work to keep the thickness of the garment even.
● The sleeves are knitted on a circular needle and worked from shoulder to cuff, so remember to reverse the order of the pattern, that is, you work from row 20 to row 1.
● When knitting in the round, loop a short strand of brightly colored wool around the first stitch each time you begin a round so that you can find the beginning easily.
● When working fronts and back the "dots" on row 20 of pattern should be worked in the same color as the "dots" on rows 1–8 of following pattern, as they are part of same color panel.

## INSTRUCTIONS

### FRONTS AND BACK

With size 2 (2¼ mm) needles, cast on 264 sts. Work 30 rows in k1 p1 rib, changing colors every 3 rows. Change to size 3 (3¼ mm) needles and work straight until 3 complete panels and 14 rows have been worked.

### Divide for fronts and back

**Row 15** With right side facing, patt 53, turn and leave rem sts on a spare needle. Work straight on these 53 sts until rows 16–20 of chart, 1 complete panel, and rows 1–8 (33 rows in all) have been worked.

### Neck shaping

**Row 9** With right side facing, bind off 7 sts, patt to end (46 sts).
**Rows 10–18** dec 1 st at neck edge every row (37 sts), then work 3 rows in background color and slip sts onto a st holder for shoulder grafting.
Return to rem 211 sts. With right side facing slip next 24 sts onto a st holder for right underarm, patt 110 sts, then turn. Work straight in patt on these 110 sts until rows 16–20 of chart, 1 complete panel, and rows 1–12 have been worked.
**Row 13** patt 44 sts, k2 tog, turn and work on these 45 sts.
**Rows 14–18** dec 1 st at neck edge every row.
**Next 3 rows** work in background colour, dec 1 st at neck edge each row (37 sts). Slip sts on to st holder for shoulder grafting.
With right side facing slip next 18 sts onto a st holder for back neck, then work rem 46 sts as follows:
**Row 13** k2 tog, patt to end.
**Rows 14–18** dec 1 st at neck edge every row.
**Next 3 rows** work in background color, dec 1 st at neck edge of each row (37 sts). Slip sts onto st holder for shoulder grafting.
Return to rem 77 sts, and with right side facing slip next 24 sts onto a st holder for left underarm, then work straight on rem 53 sts until rows 15–20 of chart, 1 complete panel, and rows 1–9 have been worked.
**Row 10** With wrong side facing bind off 7 sts, patt to end (46 sts)
**Rows 11–18** dec 1 st at neck edge every row, then work 3 rows in background color, dec 1 st at neck edge on first of these rows (37 sts). Leave sts on needle for shoulder grafting.

### Shoulder seams

Block (see page 155) garment and press carefully on wrong side using a damp cloth. With size 3 (3¼ mm) needles and wool in matching color, graft (see page 155) right front shoulder to right back shoulder (right sides together). Rep for left shoulder. Weave in any loose ends using a darning needle (do not just cut them off).

### SLEEVES

**Remember** sleeves are worked from shoulder to cuff.

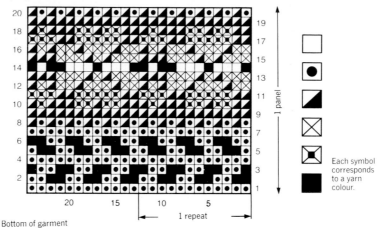

Top of garment

1 panel

Each symbol corresponds to a yarn colour.

Bottom of garment
Odd-numbered rows are knit, worked from right to left.    Even-numbered rows are purl, worked from left to right.

All rounds are k and chart is worked in rev order, from row 20–1.
With right side facing and size 3 (3¼ mm) circular needle and same background color as row 9 of 6th panel of fronts and back, slip last 12 sts from st holder onto needle and k them, pick up and k 48 sts up side of armhole to shoulder seam, 48 sts down side of armhole to st holder, then slip rem 12 sts from st holder onto needle and k them (120 sts).
**Next round** k.
**Next round** k, then, beg at row 19, work 4 panels and rows 20–10 as chart.
Change to set of 4 double-pointed size 2 (2¼ mm) needles.
**Dec round 1** *k1, k2 tog; rep from * around (80 sts).
**Dec round 2** *k2, k2 tog; rep from * around (60 sts).
Work 30 rounds in k1 p1 rib, changing color every 3 rounds and working in rev order to match Welt. Join on 2nd strand and using yarn double bind off loosely in rib. Weave in any loose ends using a darning needle (do not just cut them off) and press carefully on wrong side using a damp cloth, but do not press ribbing.

### BUTTONHOLE BAND

With right side facing and size 2 (2¼ mm) needles and same color as 1st 3 rows of welt, pick up and k 132 sts up right front edge.
**Rows 1–3** work in k1 p1 rib, then make buttonholes:
**Row 4** join on 2nd color, same as 2nd color of welt, rib 7, bind off 5 sts, *rib 20, bind off 5 sts; rep from * to last 20 sts, rib 20.
**Row 5** cont in k1 p1 rib, casting on 5 sts over the 5 buttonholes.
**Row 6** work in k1 p1 rib.
**Rows 7–9** join on 3rd color, same as 3rd color of welt, then work in k1 p1 rib.
**Row 10** p (to make foldline).
**Rows 11–13** work in k1 p1 rib.
**Row 14** join on 2nd color, same as 2nd color of welt, then work in k1 p1 rib.
**Rows 15 and 16** as rows 4 and 5.

**Rows 17–19** join on 1st color, same as 1st color of welt, work in k1 p1 rib, then bind off loosely in rib. Fold band to inside along foldline and stitch down neatly, neatening around buttonholes using a small buttonhole st.

### BUTTON BAND

With right side facing and size 2 (2¼ mm) needles and 1st color, pick up and k 132 sts down left front edge. Work 3 rows in k1 p1 rib, join on 2nd color and work 3 rows in k1 p1 rib, join on 3rd color and work 3 rows in k1 p1 rib, p next row (to make foldline), work 3 rows in k1 p1 rib, join on 2nd color and work 3 rows in k1 p1 rib, join on 1st color and work 3 rows in k1 p1 rib, then bind off loosely in rib. Fold band to inside along foldline and stitch down neatly. Sew on buttons.

### NECKBAND

With right side facing and size 2 (2¼ mm) needles and same color as 1st 3 rows of welt, pick up and k 30 sts along top edge of buttonhole band and up right front neck edge (right side facing), 12 sts down right back neck edge, 18 sts from st holder, pick up and k 12 sts up left back neck edge, 30 sts down left front neck edge and along top edge of button band (102 sts).
**Rows 1–3** work 3 rows in k1 p1 rib in 1st color.
**Row 4** join on 2nd color, rib 3, bind off 5, then rib to end.
**Row 5** cont in k1 p1 rib to last 3 sts, casting on 5 sts over buttonhole, rib 3.
**Row 6** work in k1 p1 rib.
**Rows 7–9** join on 3rd color and work in k1 p1 rib.
**Row 10** p (to make foldline).
**Rows 11–13** work in k1 p1 rib.
**Rows 14–15** join on 2nd color and work as rows 4–5.
**Row 16** Work in k1 p1 rib.
**Rows 17–19** join on 1st color, work in k1 p1 rib, then bind off loosely in rib.
Fold band to inside along foldline and stitch down neatly, neatening around buttonholes using a small buttonhole stitch.

# AMERICAN LEAF CARDIGAN

Early settlers in North America found the winters cold and fabrics in short supply. Housewives saved worn-out clothes, which were cut up, arranged into simple patterns, lined with padding, and stitched to form a quilt. This is recycling at its best: frugal, unpretentious, and capable of creating really stunning works of art. I have always adored patchwork quilts. An American friend gave me one that had been used by her grandmother as an under blanket and was entirely made out of men's work shirts. Our own bedspread was made by the wife of a Durham miner about a century ago. In both cases, the lack of an educated approach to design has produced an original and free piece of work. The American Leaf cardigan was born out of my love of quilts, and takes its inspiration from the decorative border that usually surrounds the main design.

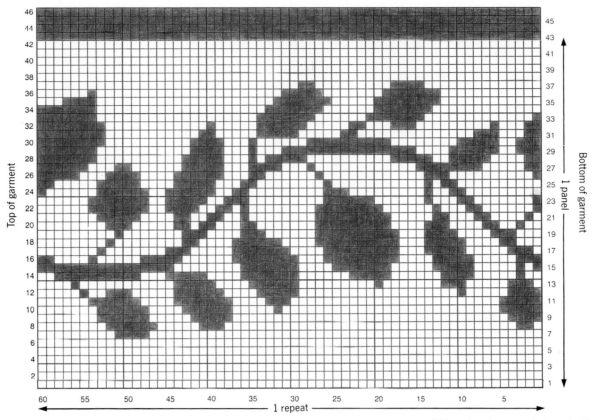

*Odd-numbered rows are knit, worked from right to left.*
*Even-numbered rows are purl, worked from left to right.*

## MATERIALS

Pair of size 2 (2¼ mm) needles
Set of 4 double-pointed size 2 (2¼ mm) needles
Pair of size 3 (3¼ mm) needles
7 buttons

## WEIGHT OF YARN AND COLORS

**1. Red, white, and blue**
**Navy (A)** 16 oz (460 g)
**Natural (B)** 8 oz (230 g)
**Crimson (C)** 12 oz (340 g)

**2. Navy, blue, and white**
**Navy (A)** 16 oz (460 g)
**Natural (B)** 8 oz (230 g)
**Dark indigo blue (C)** 12 oz (340 g)

## MEASUREMENTS

Length from shoulder to bottom edge of cardigan:
24 in (61 cm)
Actual width all around at underarm: 58 in (147 cm)
Sleeve length: 20 in (51 cm)

## GAUGE

Over pattern, using size 3 (3¼ mm) needles (or size to obtain gauge), 30 stitches and 30 rows to 4 in (10 cm)

## IMPORTANT

● Twist wools at back of work every 1–2 stitches to avoid making holes, but do not pull tight.
● When working St st using just one color, twist a spare ball of the same color yarn across the back of work to keep the thickness of the garment even.
● This garment is knitted sideways, beginning at the left front edge, and the sleeves are also knitted sideways.
● Before beginning each new panel, check with the diagram below to ensure that you have the correct color combination.

Key
**X** = background A, leaf B and stem C.
**Y** = background C, leaf A and stem B.
**Z** = background B, leaf C and stem A.

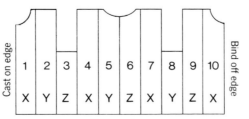

## INSTRUCTIONS
### FRONTS AND BACK

**Panel 1**
With size 3 (3¼ mm) needles and color combination X, cast on 126 sts in A and work from chart, beg at st 1, row 1.
**Rows 1–12** as chart.
**Neck shaping**
**Row 13** With right side facing inc 1 st at end (neck edge) of row.
**Rows 14–16** as chart.
**Rows 17–29** inc 1 st at end (neck edge) of this and next 6 alternate rows (134 sts).
**Rows 30–31** as chart.
**Row 32** With wrong side facing cast on 15 sts (neck edge), patt to end (149 sts).
**Rows 33–42** as chart, then work 4 rows rev St st in A as follows:
**Row 1** k.
**Row 2** k.
**Row 3** p.
**Row 4** k.

**Panel 2**
Using color combination Y, work from chart.
**Rows 1–41** as chart.

**Row 42** With wrong side facing, bind off 52 sts (neck edge), patt to end (97 sts), then join on A and work 4 rows rev St st as before.

**Panel 3** (underarm panel)
Using color combination Z, work from chart.
**Rows 1–42** as chart, then join on A and work 4 rows rev St st as before.

**Panel 4**
Using color combination X, work from chart.
**Row 1** With right side facing, patt to end of row (neck edge), then cast on 52 sts (149 sts).
**Rows 2–42** as chart, then work 4 rows rev St st in A as before.

**Panel 5**
Using color combination Y, work from chart.
**Rows 1–10** as chart.
**Rows 11–15** dec 1 st at end (neck edge) of this and next 2 alternate rows (146 sts).
**Rows 16–42** as chart, then join on A and work 4 rows rev St st as before.

**Panel 6**
Using color combination Z, work from chart.
**Rows 1–26** as chart.
**Rows 27–31** inc 1 st at end (neck edge) of this and next 2 alternate rows (149 sts).
**Rows 32–42** as chart, then join on A and work 4 rows rev St st as before.

**Panel 7**
Using color combination X, work from chart.
**Rows 1–41** as chart.
**Row 42** With wrong side facing bind off 52 sts (neck edge), patt to end (97 sts), then work 4 rows rev St st in A as before.

**Panel 8** (underarm panel)
Using color combination Y, work from chart.
**Rows 1–42** as chart, then join on A and work 4 rows rev St st as before.

**Panel 9**
Using color combination Z, work from chart.
**Row 1** With right side facing patt to end of row (neck edge), then cast on 52 sts (149 sts).
**Rows 2–42** as chart, then join on A and work 4 rows rev St st as before.

**Panel 10**
Using color combination X, work from chart.
**Rows 1–11** as chart.
Neck shaping
**Row 12** With wrong side facing, bind off 15 sts, patt to end (134 sts).

**Rows 13–14** as chart.
**Rows 15–27** dec 1 st at end (neck edge) of this and next 6 alternate rows (127 sts).
**Rows 28–30** as chart.
**Row 31** dec 1 st at end (neck edge) of row (126 sts).
**Rows 32–42** as chart, then bind off loosely.
Weave in any loose ends using a darning needle (do not just cut them off). Block (see page 155) garment and press carefully on wrong side using a damp cloth.

**Shoulder seams**
With right side facing and size 2 (2¼ mm) needles and A, pick up and k 52 sts along right front shoulder. K 1 row, p 1 row, k 1 row. Leave sts on a spare needle for grafting. With right side facing and size 2 (2¼ mm) needles and A, pick up and k 52 sts along right back shoulder and leave sts on needle for grafting. Graft (see page 155) right front shoulder to right back shoulder (right sides together). Rep for left shoulder.

**SLEEVES**
**Left sleeve**
With size 3 (3¼ mm) needles and B, cast on 123 sts. Work 6 complete panels with 4 rows rev St st in A between each panel with colour combinations in following order:
Panel 1 (underarm panel) Z.
Panel 2 X.
Panel 3 Y.
Panel 4 Z.
Panel 5 X.
Panel 6 Y.
Then work 4 rows rev St st in A and keep sts on needle. Weave in any loose ends using a darning needle (do not just cut them off). Press carefully on wrong side using a damp cloth, then graft (see page 155) cast-on edge to sts on needle.

**Right sleeve**
Work as left sleeve, but in following color combinations:
Panel 1 (underarm panel) Y.
Panel 2 Z.
Panel 3 X.
Panel 4 Y.
Panel 5 Z.
Panel 6 X.

**Cuffs**
With right side facing and set of 4 double-pointed size 2 (2¼ mm) needles and A, pick up and k 160 sts around lower edge of sleeve (making sure leaves are pointing down to cuff). Loop a short strand of brightly colored wool around 1st st of each round so that you can find beg of round easily.
**Round 1** *k2 tog; rep from * around (80 sts).
**Round 2** *k2, k2 tog; rep from * around (60 sts).

Work 32 rounds in k1 p1 rib, then join on 2nd strand A and using yarn double bind off loosely in rib.

**WELT**
With right side facing and size 2 (2¼ mm) needles and A, pick up and k 230 sts along lower edge of fronts and back. Work 32 rows in k1 p1 rib, then join on 2nd strand A and using yarn double bind off loosely in rib.

**NECKBAND**
With right side facing and size 2 (2¼ mm) needles and A, pick up and k 100 sts around neck. Work 9 rows in k1 p1 rib, k 2 rows (to make foldline), then work 9 rows more in k1 p1 rib. Bind off loosely in rib.

**BUTTONHOLE BAND**
With right side facing and size 2 (2¼ mm) needles and A, pick up and k 180 sts up right front edge.
**Rows 1–4** work in k1 p1 rib, then make buttonholes.
**Row 5** rib 6, *bind off 6 sts, rib 21 including st already on needle; rep from * to last 12 sts, bind off 6 sts, rib 6.
**Row 6** work in k1 p1 rib, casting on 6 sts over the 7 buttonholes.
**Rows 7–9** work in k1 p1 rib.
**Rows 10 and 11** k (to make foldline).
**Rows 12–14** work in k1 p1 rib.
**Rows 15 and 16** as rows 5 and 6.
**Rows 17–20** work in k1 p1 rib, then bind off loosely in rib. Fold band to inside along foldline and stitch down neatly, neatening around buttonholes using a small buttonhole st.

**BUTTON BAND**
With right side facing and size 2 (2¼ mm) needles and A, pick up and k 180 sts down left front edge. Work 9 rows in k1 p1 rib, k 2 rows (to make foldline), then work 9 more rows in k1 p1 rib and bind off loosely in rib. Fold band to inside along foldline and stitch down neatly. Sew on buttons.

**SLEEVE INSERTION**
Make 3 pleats in top of left sleeve by folding rev St st at top edge of panel 5 to center of panel 5; rev St st at top edge of panel 4 to center of panel 4; and rev St st at top edge of panel 3 to center of panel 3. On right sleeve fold rev St st at top edge of panel 2 to center of panel 3; panel 3 to panel 4; and panel 4 to panel 5. Stitch the pleats down neatly (check that pleats face front of garment and that underarm panel is in the same color combination as underarm panel on body). With right side facing and set of 4 double-pointed size 2 (2¼ mm) needles and A, pick up and k 110 sts around top edge of sleeve and p 3 rounds. Leave sts on needle. Place sleeve in armhole (right sides together), matching underarm panels and middle pleat with shoulder seam, and graft (see page 155) tog. Weave in any rem loose ends using a darning needle (do not just cut them off).

# PLAITED BAND

## MATERIALS
Pair of size 5 (4½ mm) needles
3 strips approximately 3 ft 4 in by 2¼ in (100 by 6 cm)
of 4 oz (115 g) polyester padding

## WEIGHT OF YARN AND COLORS
Natural (A)   2 oz (57 g)
Navy (B)   2 oz (57 g)
Crimson (C)   2 oz (57 g)

## GAUGE
Over stockinette stitch, using size 5 (4½ mm) needles
(or size to obtain gauge), 25 stitches and 24 rows to 4
in (10 cm).

## INSTRUCTIONS

## BAND 1
With size 5 (4½ mm) needles and A, cast on 112 sts.
Work 26 rows in St st, then bind off loosely.

## BAND 2
As band 1, but work in B.

## BAND 3
As band 1, but work in C.
Weave in any loose ends on all bands using a darning
needle (do not just cut them off), then press on wrong
side using a damp cloth.

## FINISHING
Lay band 1 (wrong side up) on a flat surface and lay one
of the strips of padding down the center.
Bring each side of band up over padding to meet along
center and oversew edges neatly in A.
Rep these 2 stages for bands 2 and 3, oversewing in B
and C respectively.
Then braid the bands tog – firmly but not too tightly –
and bring ends of braid tog to form a circle.
Stitch ends of padding tog, then oversew ends of band
1 tog neatly and rep for bands 2 and 3. Adjust braid so
that seams are inside or under another band.

# PAISLEY JACKET

A longtime favorite and a true classic. The paisley motif combines a floral design from woven Indian shawls, a Persian vase of flowers, and, less exotically, the stylized pine pattern used on the shawls produced in the Scottish town of Paisley in the 19th century. Despite the apparent simplicity, it was difficult to translate onto graph paper in a way that would be easy to knit, and I spent hours drawing paisley designs before finding one that worked well on a jacket. I have used three colors in a row, and it is important to keep the tension even and weave the wool on every stitch. The navy background can be dyed in one go by multiplying the recipe by five.

## MATERIALS

Pair of size 2 (2¼ mm) needles
Set of 4 double-pointed size 2 (2¼ mm) needles
Pair of size 3 (3¼ mm) needles
Circular size 3 (3¼ mm) needle 16 in (40 cm) long
9 stitch holders
7 buttons

## WEIGHT OF YARN AND COLORS

**Navy (A)**  20 oz (560 g)
**Crimson (B1)**  8 oz (230 g)
**Red (B2)**  8 oz (230 g)
**Grass green (C)**  6 oz (170 g)

## MEASUREMENTS

Length from top of shoulder to bottom edge of jacket:
34 in (86.5 cm)
Actual width all around at underarm: 50 in (127 cm)
Sleeve length: 22½ in (57 cm)

## GAUGE

Over pattern, using size 3 (3¼ mm) needles (or size to obtain gauge), 30 stitches and 28 rows to 4 in (10 cm).

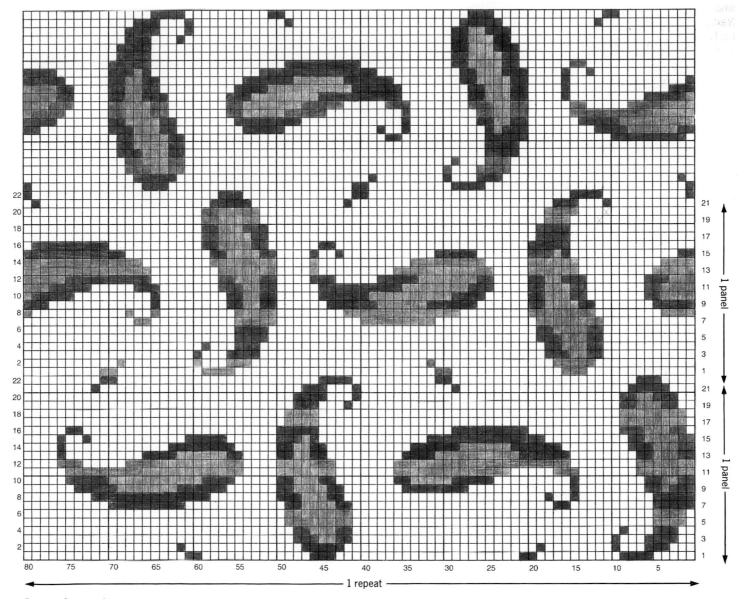

Bottom of garment

— 1 repeat —

Odd-numbered rows are knit, worked from right to left.
Even-numbered rows are purl, worked from left to right.

## IMPORTANT

● The pattern is staggered, therefore begin panel 1 at stitch 1, row 1; panel 2 at stitch 31, row 1; panel 3 at stitch 61, row 1; panel 4 at stitch 11, row 1; panel 5 at stitch 41, row 1; panel 6 at stitch 71, row 1; panel 7 at stitch 21, row 1; panel 8 at stitch 51, row 1; panel 9 as panel 1 and so on (chart shows the first 3 panels).

● Change shade of red every 2–3 rows to give a random effect.

● Twist wools at back of work every 1–2 stitches to avoid making holes, but do not pull tight.

● When working St st using just one color twist a spare ball of the same color yarn across the back of work to keep the thickness of the garment even.

● When using the circular needle for the sleeves, remember that all rounds of chart are knit and must be worked in reverse order as you are knitting from shoulder to cuff, that is, you work from row 22 to 1.

● When using the circular needle, loop a short strand of brightly colored wool around the first stitch each time you begin a round so that you can find the beginning easily.

## INSTRUCTIONS
### FRONTS AND BACK

With size 2 (2¼ mm) needles and 2 strands A (to give a firmer edge), cast on 310 sts. Cont with 1 strand A and work in k1 p1 rib as follows:

**Rows 1–4** work in A.
**Rows 5–8** work in B.
**Rows 9 and 10** work in C.
**Rows 11–14** work in B.
**Rows 15–16** work in A.
**Rows 17–20** work in C.
**Rows 21–22** work in B.
**Rows 23–26** work in C.
**Rows 27–28** work in A.
**Rows 29–32** work in B.
**Rows 33–34** work in C.
**Rows 35–38** work in B.
**Rows 39–41** work in A.

**Next row** (wrong side facing) *rib 4, inc into next st; rep from * to end (372 sts).

**Next row** change to size 3 (3¼ mm) needles, k1, then work from chart, beg at st 1, row 1, to last st, k1. (Omit

small motifs on 1st 2 rows.)
**Next row** p 1, patt to last st, p1.
Cont as chart, keeping 1st and last sts plain as these are the front edges, and work 2 complete panels (44 rows).

### Pocket linings

Lay work aside. With size 3 (3¼ mm) needles and A, cast on 42 sts. For pocket lining 1, beg at st 28, row 1 of chart, for pocket lining 2, beg at st 62, row 1 and work 2 complete panels. Leave sts on spare needles. Return to main body of work. Patt 28 sts, slip next 42 sts onto a st holder for pocket top, then join in pocket lining 1, k from its needle, keeping patt correct, and patt to last 70 sts. Slip next 42 sts onto a st holder for pocket top, then join in pocket lining 2, k from its needle, keeping patt correct, and patt to end. Work straight until 6 complete panels have been worked.

### Divide for fronts and back

With right side facing patt 70 sts, turn. Cont in patt on these 70 sts until 8 complete panels have been worked from beg.
**Next row** bind off 16 sts for neck, patt to end (54 sts).
**Next row** row 2 of chart.
**Row 3** bind off 2 sts, patt to end.
**Row 4** as chart.
**Row 5** bind off 2 sts, patt to end.
**Row 6** as chart.
**Rows 7–17** dec 1 st at beg (neck edge) of this and next 5 alternate rows (44 sts).
Work straight in patt until 9 panels have been worked from beg, then slip sts onto a st holder for right shoulder grafting. Return to rem sts, slip next 46 sts onto a st holder for right underarm, then patt next 140 sts for back and turn. Work straight on these 140 sts until 8 complete panels and 14 rows have been worked from beg.
**Next row** With right side facing patt 49, k2 tog, k1, turn.
**Next row** p1, p2 tog, patt to end.
**Next row** patt to last 3 sts, k2 tog, k1.
Rep last 2 rows until 44 sts rem (9 complete panels have now been worked), then slip sts onto a st holder for right back shoulder grafting. Slip next 36 sts onto a st holder for back neck and work rem 52 sts as follows: k1, k2 tog, patt to end.
**Next row** patt to last 3 sts, p2 tog, p1.
**Next row** k1, k2 tog, patt to end.
Rep last 2 rows until 44 sts rem (9 complete panels have now been worked), then slip sts onto a st holder for left back shoulder grafting. Slip next 46 sts onto a st holder for left underarm and then patt rem 70 sts.
Work straight on these sts until 8 complete panels and 1 row of chart have been worked from beg.
**Row 2** bind off 16 sts, patt to end (54 sts).
**Row 3** as chart.
**Row 4** bind off 2 sts, patt to end.
**Row 5** as chart.
**Row 6** bind off 2 sts, patt to end.

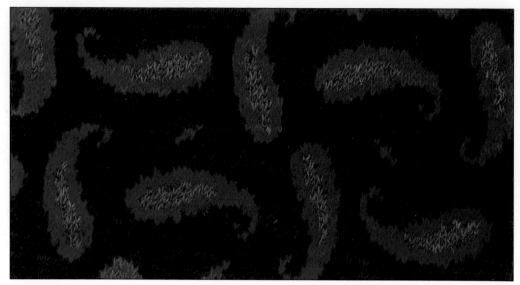

**Row 7** as chart.
**Rows 8–18** dec 1 st at beg (neck edge) of this and next 5 alternate rows (44 sts).
Work straight in patt until 9 complete panels have been worked, then slip sts onto a st holder for left front shoulder grafting.

### Pocket tops

With right side facing and size 2 (2¼ mm) needles and A, slip sts for pocket from st holder onto needle and work in k1 p1 rib as follows:
**Rows 1 and 2** work in A.
**Rows 3–6** work in B.
**Rows 7 and 8** work in C.
**Rows 9–10** work in B.
**Rows 11 and 12** work in A, then bind off loosely in rib using 2 strands A. Block (see page 155) garment and press carefully on wrong side using a damp cloth, but do not press ribbing. Stitch down pocket tops neatly and sew pocket linings into place using a small slip st.

### Shoulder seams

Graft (see page 155) right front shoulder to right back shoulder (right sides together). Rep for other shoulder. Press carefully on wrong side using a damp cloth, but do not press ribbing.

### SLEEVES

**Remember** to k all rounds and work panels in rev order – from row 22–1.
With right side facing and a size 3 (3¼ mm) circular needle and A, slip last 23 sts for underarm from st holder onto needle and k them. Then pick up and k 114 sts around armhole and k rem 23 sts from st holder (160 sts). Working from chart in rev order, cont until 6 panels have been worked. Cont with A.
**Next round** *k2, k2 tog; rep from * around (120 sts).
**Next round** change to set of 4 double-pointed size 2 (2¼ mm) needles and *k2 tog; rep from * around (60

sts). Then work 45 rounds in k1 p1 rib following color sequence of rib given at beg of instructions for fronts and back, but in rev order and working 4 rows instead of 2 in the A stripes. Bind off in rib using 2 strands A. Weave in any loose ends using a darning needle (do not just cut them off) and press carefully on wrong side using a damp cloth, but do not press ribbing.

### NECKBAND

With right side facing and size 2 (2¼ mm) needles and A, pick up and k 110 sts around neck, including sts on holder at back neck. Working in k1 p1 rib work 2 rows A, 4 rows B, 2 rows C, 4 rows B and 2 rows A then bind off loosely in rib using 2 strands A.

### BUTTONHOLE BAND

With right side facing and size 2 (2¼ mm) needles and A, pick up and k 210 sts up right front edge of jacket.
**Rows 1 and 2** work in k1 p1 rib in A.
**Rows 3–6** work in k1 p1 rib in B, then make buttonholes:
**Row 7** working in C, rib 3, bind off 6 sts, *rib 27, including st left on needle, bind off 6; rep from * to last 3 sts, rib 3.
**Row 8** cont in C in k1 p1 rib, casting on 6 sts over the 7 buttonholes.
**Rows 9–12** work in k1 p1 rib in B.
**Rows 13 and 14** work in k1 p1 rib in A, then bind off loosely in rib using 2 strands A.
Using a strand of C, neaten around buttonholes using a small buttonhole st.

### BUTTON BAND

With right side facing and size 2 (2¼ mm) needles and A, pick up and k 210 sts down left front edge of jacket. Work in k1 p1 rib as given for rows 1–14 of neckband above. Bind off loosely in rib using 2 strands A. Sew on buttons.

# PAISLEY HAT

## MATERIALS

Pair of size 8 (5 mm) needles
size H (4 mm) crochet hook
Approximately 4 ft by 4 in (130 by 10 cm) strip of 4 oz (115 g) polyester padding

## WEIGHT OF YARN AND COLORS

PLIED YARN    (or 2 strands of ordinary yarn knitted together)
Navy (A)    4 oz (115 g)
Grass green (B)    4 oz (115 g)
Crimson (C)    4 oz (115 g)

## GAUGE

Over pattern, using size 8 (5 mm) needles (or size to obtain gauge), 16 stitches and 24 rows to 4in (10 cm).

## INSTRUCTIONS
### BRIM

With size 8 (5 mm) needles and A, cast on 60 sts. Work in St st.
**Row 1** k.
**Row 2** p.
**Row 3** join on B, inc 1 st at beg of row and dec 1 st at end of row.
**Row 4** p.
**Rows 5–9** Rep rows 3 and 4 twice and row 3 once.
**Row 10** join on A and p.
**Rows 11–17** join on C and shape as rows 3 and 4.
Rows 2–17 form stripe pattern. Rep 4 more times and then bind off loosely. Weave in any loose ends using a darning needle (do not just cut them off) and press carefully on wrong side using a damp cloth. Bring cast-on edge and bound-off edge tog (right sides tog) and sew neat seam using small backstitches.

### CROWN

With right side facing and size 8 (5 mm) needles and A, cast on 104 sts and work 22 rows in St st, then shape as follows:
**Row 1** k5, k3 tog, *k10, k3 tog; rep from * to last 5 sts, k5 (88 sts).
**Rows 2–6** work in St st.
**Row 7** k4, k3 tog, *k8, k3 tog; rep from * to last 4 sts, k4 (72 sts).
**Rows 8–12** work in St st.
**Row 13** k3, k3 tog, *k6, k3 tog; rep from * to last 3 sts, k3 (56 sts).
**Rows 14–18** work in St st.
**Row 19** k2, k3 tog, *k4, k3 tog; rep from * to last 2 sts, k2 (40 sts).
**Rows 20–25** work in St st.
**Row 26** k1, k3 tog, *k2, k3 tog; rep from * to last st, k1 (24 sts).
**Row 27** *k2 tog; rep from * to end (12 sts). Keep sts

on needle. Cut off wool, leaving a length of about 5¾ in (15 cm), then, using a darning needle, thread this through sts on needle, pull tightly and fasten off securely. Bring side edges of crown tog (right sides tog) and sew neat seam using small backstitches.

### FLAPS
### Right flap lining

With size 8 (5 mm) needles and B, cast on 30 sts and work 100 rows in st st.
**Next row** *k3 tog; rep from * to end of row (10 sts). Cut off wool, leaving a length of about 5¾ in (15 cm), then, using a darning needle, thread this through sts on needle, pull tightly and fasten off securely. Rep for left flap lining, but work in C.

### Right outer flap

With size 8 (5 mm) needles and A, cast on 30 sts and work 100 rows as chart.
**Next row** *k3 tog; rep to end of row (10 sts). Fasten off as flap linings above. Rep for left outer flap.

### FINISHING
### Flaps

Place right outer flap on right flap lining (right sides tog) and sew neat seam using small backstitches all around flap, except for cast-on edges, then turn right side out and stitch cast-on edges of each flap tog neatly. Rep for left outer flap and left flap lining.

### Tassels

(See page 157 for Crochet instructions.) With size H (4mm) crochet hook and A, make 2 braids 40 ch in length. Cut 60 lengths of B and 60 lengths of C, each approximately 11¾ in (30 cm) long.
Fold the 60 lengths of B over the center of one of the crocheted braids, then wind a strand of B several times tightly around lengths of B, forming tassel, and tie a tight knot. With a strand of A, stitch the crocheted braid immediately above top of tassel. Then pass the 2 ends of the crocheted braid through the small hole at the gathered end of the flap and stitch firmly in place on wrong side. Rep for 2nd tassel in C.

### Joining brim and crown

Place edge of brim approximately 3¼ in (2 cm) above cast-on edge of crown (right sides tog) and stitch a neat seam using small backstitches. Place right flap 2 in (5 cm) away from seam in crown (lining and wrong side of crown tog, cast-on edges aligned) and sew neat seam using small backstitches. Rep for left flap.
Fold padding in half lengthwise and lay it on wrong side of brim below seam. Bring unsewn edge of brim down over padding and slip stitch it carefully to cast-on edge of crown and right side of flaps, turning edge of brim under as you do so for a neat finish.

Cast off edge

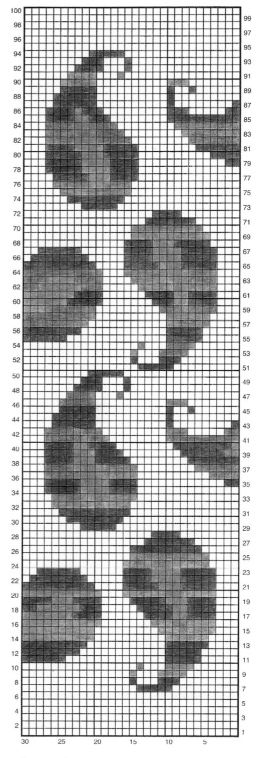

Cast on edge
Odd-numbered rows are knit, worked from right to left.
Even-numbered rows are purl, worked from left to right.

# FOUR-LEAF CLOVER JACKET

"With a four leav'd clover, double topp'd ash, and green tipp'd seave
You may go before the queen's daughter without ever asking leave."

Ash and green rushes are no longer thought of as lucky, but the four-leaf clover remains as strong a symbol of good fortune as ever. As a family, we always hunt for one when in a meadow or on a picnic, and the thrill of discovery is as memorable now as it was when I was a child.

The clovers climb the cardigan, and the natural greens blend together in infinite variations. The dark gray ruffles dividing the panels create a rippled effect against the gray background. It is possible to dye all the 16 oz (460 g) of gray needed in one go by using a larger saucepan and multiplying the quantities of dye and mordant given in the recipe by four.

## MATERIALS

Pair of size 2 (2¼ mm) needles
Set of 4 double-pointed size 2 (2¼ mm) needles
Pair of size 3 (3¼ mm) needles
Set of 4 double-pointed size 3 (3¼ mm) needles
6 buttons

## WEIGHT OF YARN AND COLORS

**Gray (A)**   16 oz (460 g)
**Dark gray (B)**   6 oz (170 g)
**Grass green (C1)**   4 oz (115 g)
**Olive green (C2)**   4 oz (115 g)
**Blue-green (C3)**   4 oz (115 g)

## MEASUREMENTS

Length from top of shoulder to bottom edge of jacket:
27 in (68.5 cm)
Actual width all around at underarm: 50 in (127 cm)
Sleeve length: 22½ in (57 cm)

## GAUGE

Over pattern, using size 3 (3¼ mm) needles (or size to obtain gauge), 28 sts and 28 rows to 4 in (10 cm).

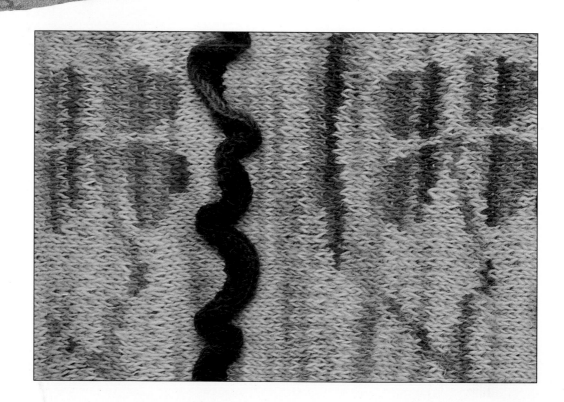

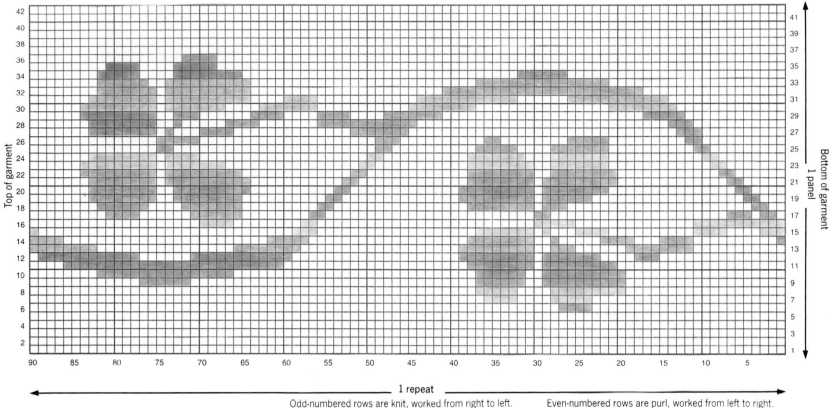

Top of garment

Bottom of garment
1 panel

1 repeat

Odd-numbered rows are knit, worked from right to left.     Even-numbered rows are purl, worked from left to right.

## IMPORTANT

- Twist wools at back of work every 1–2 stitches to avoid making holes, but do not pull tight.
- When working St st using just one color, twist a spare ball of the same color yarn across the back of work to keep the thickness of the garment even.
- Change colors of four-leaf clover motif every 2–3 rows to give a random effect.
- This garment is knitted sideways, beginning at the left front edge, and the sleeves are also knitted sideways.
- The frills are added after the fronts and back and the sleeves have been worked.

## INSTRUCTIONS
### FRONTS AND BACK

**Panel 1**

With size 3 (3¼ mm) needles and A, cast on 146 sts.

**Row 1** (right side facing) k.

**Row 2** p.

**Row 3** work from chart, beg at st 1, row 21.

**Rows 22–26** as chart.

Cont working from chart, inc on each alternate row as follows:

**Rows 27 and 29** inc 1 st at end (neck edge) of row.

**Rows 31 and 33** cast on 2 sts at end (neck edge) of row.

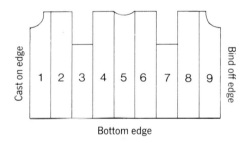

Cast on edge

Bind off edge

1  2  3  4  5  6  7  8  9

Bottom edge

**Rows 35 and 37** cast on 3 sts at end (neck edge) of row.

**Rows 39 and 41** cast on 5 sts at end (neck edge) of row (168 sts)

**Row 42** as chart, then join on B, k 2 rows and cut off B.

**Panel 2**

Cont in A and work from chart, beg at st 1, row 1.

**Rows 1–41** as chart.

**Row 42** With wrong side facing bind off 52 sts (neck edge), patt to end (116 sts), then join on B, k 2 rows and cut off B.

**Panel 3** (underarm panel)

Cont in A and work rows 1–42 as chart, beg at st 1, row 1, then join on B, k 2 rows and cut off B.

**Panel 4**

Cont in A and work from chart, beg at st 1, row 1.

**Row 1** Patt to end of row (neck edge), then cast on 52 sts (168 sts).

**Rows 2–42** as chart, then join on B, k 2 rows and cut off B.

**Panel 5**

Cont in A and work from chart, beg at st 1, row 1, dec and inc as follows:

**Row 1** With right side facing dec 1 st at end (neck edge) of row.

**Row 4** dec 1 st at beg (neck edge) of row.

**Row 8** dec 1 st at beg (neck edge) of row.

**Row 12** dec 1 st at beg (neck edge) of row.

**Rows 13–29** work straight as chart.

**Row 30** With wrong side facing inc 1 st at beg (neck edge) of row.

**Row 34** inc 1 st at beg (neck edge) of row.

**Row 38** inc 1 st at beg (neck edge) of row.

**Row 42** inc 1 st at beg (neck edge) of row (168 sts), then join on B, k 2 rows and cut off B.

**Panel 6**

Cont in A and work from chart, beg at st 1, row 1.

**Rows 1–41** as chart.

**Row 42** bind off 52 sts (neck edge), patt to end (116 sts), then join on B, k 2 rows and cut off B.

**Panel 7** (underarm panel)

Cont in A and work from chart, beg at st 1, row 1.

**Rows 1–42** as chart, then join on B, k 2 rows and cut off B.

**Panel 8**

Cont in A and work from chart, beg at st 1, row 1.

**Row 1** Patt to end of row (neck edge), then cast on 52 sts (168 sts).

**Rows 2–42** as chart, then join on B, k 2 rows and cut off B.

**Panel 9**

Cont in A and work from chart, beg at st 1, row 1, dec on each alternate row as follows:

**Rows 2 and 4** bind off 5 sts (neck edge), patt to end.

**Rows 6 and 8** bind off 3 sts (neck edge), patt to end.

**Rows 10 and 12** bind off 2 sts (neck edge), patt to end.

**Rows 14 and 16** bind off 1 st (neck edge), patt to end (146 sts).

**Rows 17–22** as chart. With A, k 1 row, p 1 row, then bind off loosely. Weave in any loose ends using a darning needle (do not just cut them off), then block (see page 155) garment and press carefully on wrong side using a damp cloth.

**Frills**

With right side facing and size 2 (2¼ mm) needles and B, pick up and k 168 sts along 2 k rows in B between panels 1 and 2. Work 2 rows in k1 p1 rib, then change to size 3 (3¼ mm) needles and work 1 row inc into every st (336 sts).

**Next row** work in k1 p1 rib.

**Next row** k, then bind off loosely purlwise.

Rep for each 2 k row in B between panels, but pick up and k 116 sts instead of 168 either side of panels 3 and 7.

**Shoulder seams**

With right side facing and size 2 (2¼ mm) needles and B, pick up and k 40 sts along right front shoulder, k 1 row and leave sts on a spare needle for grafting.

With right side facing and size 2 (2¼ mm) needles and B, pick up and k 40 sts along right back shoulder and leave sts on needle for grafting. Graft (see page 155) right front shoulder to right back shoulder (right sides tog).

**Frill** Pick up and k 40 sts (not 168) along shoulder seam and work as before.

Rep for 2nd shoulder.

Using darning needle and a short strand of B, fasten down ends of shoulder frills and frills of fronts and back by passing needle up through work, through end bound off st of frill and back through work, pulling tightly so frill curves in to work.

**SLEEVES**

With size 3 (3¼ mm) needles and A, cast on 133 sts and work 4 complete panels as chart with 2 k rows in B between each panel, ending with 2 k rows in B. Keep sts on needle. Press carefully on wrong side using a damp cloth and graft (see page 155) sts on needle to cast-on edge of sleeve (right sides together).

**Frills**

Work as before, but pick up and k 133 sts instead of 168.

**Cuffs**

With right side facing and set of 4 double-pointed size 2 (2¼ mm) needles and B, pick up and k 122 sts around lower edge of sleeve, ensuring patt is right way up. When picking up sts, pick up a st through end bound off st of each frill and pull tightly so it curves into cuff to neaten.

**Round 1** *k2 tog; rep from * around (61 sts).

**Round 2** *k4, k2 tog; rep from * to last 7 sts, k4, k3 tog (50 sts), then work 24 more rounds in k1 p1 rib. Loop a short strand of brightly colored wool around 1st st of round as a marker and then work 2 rounds in k1 p1 rib.

**Frill 1** Change to set of 4 double-pointed size 3 (3¼ mm) needles and work 1 round, inc into every st (100 sts).

**Next round** work in k1 p1 rib.

**Next round** p, then bind off loosely knitwise.

**Frill 2** With set of 4 double-pointed size 2 (2¼ mm) needles and B, pick up and k 50 sts along round indicated by marker on inside of cuff. Work 3 rounds in k1 p1 rib, then loop a short strand of brightly colored wool round 1st st of round. Work 2 more rounds in k1 p1 rib. Then change to set of 4 double-pointed size 3 (3¼ mm) needles and work 1 round, inc into every st (100 sts).

**Next round** work in k1 p1 rib.

**Next round** p, then bind off loosely knitwise.

**Frill 3** With set of 4 double-pointed size 2 (2¼ mm) needles and B, pick up and k 50 sts along round indicated by 2nd marker on inside of cuff. Work 5 rounds in k1 p1 rib, then change to set of 4 double-pointed size 3 (3¼ mm) needles and work 1 round, inc into every st (100 sts).

**Next round** work in k1 p1 rib.

**Next round** p, then bind off loosely knitwise.

**WELT**

With right side facing and size 2 (2¼ mm) needles and B, pick up and k 230 sts along lower edge of fronts and back, picking up a st through end bound off st of each frill, pulling it tightly so it curves into welt as you do so to neaten. Work 25 rows in k1 p1 rib. Join on 2nd strand B and using yarn double cast off loosely in rib.

**NECKBAND**

With right side facing and size 2 (2¼ mm) needles and B, pick up and k 110 sts around neck. Work 5 rows in k1 p1 rib.

**Frill 1** Change to size 3 (3¼mm) needles and work 1 row, inc into every st, then pick up and k 4 sts down side of ribbing (224 sts).

**Next row** work in k1 p1 rib and then pick up and k 4 sts down side of ribbing (228 sts). K 2 rows, then bind off loosely purlwise.

**Frill 2** Turn Frill 1 down on to right side of work and with size 2 (2¼ mm) needles and B, pick up and k 110 sts on inside of neck in exactly the same place as Frill 1, then work 7 rows in k1 p1 rib. Change to size 3 (3¼ mm) needles and work 1 row, inc into every st, then pick up and k 6 sts down side of ribbing (226 sts).

**Next row** work in k1 p1 rib, then pick up and k 6 sts down side of ribbing (232 sts). K 2 rows, then bind off loosely purlwise.

**Frill 3** Turn Frills 1 and 2 down on to right side of work and with size 2 (2¼ mm) needles and B, pick up and k 110 sts on inside of neck in exactly the same place as Frills 1 and 2, then work 11 rows in k1 p1 rib. Change to size 3 (3¼ mm) needles and work 1 row, inc into every st, then pick up and k 10 sts down side of ribbing (230 sts).

**Next row** work in k1 p1 rib, then pick up and k 10 sts down side of ribbing (240 sts). K 2 rows, then bind off loosely purlwise.

**BUTTONHOLE BAND**

With right side facing and size 2 (2¼ mm) needles and B, pick up and k 172 sts up right front edge.

**Rows 1–3** work in k1 p1 rib, then make buttonholes:

**Row 4** rib 3, bind off 6 sts, *rib 26 including st already on needle, bind off 6 sts; rep from * to last 3 sts, rib 3.

**Row 5** cont in k1 p1 rib, casting on 6 sts over the 6 buttonholes.

**Rows 6–9** work in k1 p1 rib.

**Row 10** p (to make foldline).

**Rows 11–14** work in k1 p1 rib.

**Rows 15 and 16** as rows 4 and 5.

**Rows 17–19** work in k1 p1 rib, then bind off loosely in rib. Fold band to inside along foldline and stitch down neatly, neatening around buttonholes using a small buttonhole st.

**BUTTON BAND**

With right side facing and size 2 (2¼ mm) needles and B, pick up and k 172 sts down left front edge. Work 9 rows in k1 p1 rib, p next row (to make foldline), work 9 more rows in k1 p1 rib, then bind off loosely in rib. Fold band to inside along foldline and stitch down neatly. Sew on buttons.

**ARMHOLE FRILLS**

With right side facing and set of 4 double-pointed size 2 (2¼ mm) needles and B, pick up and k 122 sts along 2nd row in of 3 of the panels at top of sleeve (4th panel is the underarm panel). Work 2 rows in k1 p1 rib, then change to set of 4 double-pointed size 3 (3¼ mm) needles and inc into every st (244 sts).

**Next row** work in k1 p1 rib.

**Next row** k, then bind off loosely purlwise.

**SLEEVE INSERTION**

Place sleeve in armhole with right sides tog, matching underarm panel and making sure frill is turned down on right side of sleeve. Sew neat seam using small back sts. Weave in any rem loose ends using a darning needle and press carefully on wrong side using a damp cloth. Do not press ribbing or frills.

# FRITILLARY JACKET

We live on the edge of water meadows, and the ground is always damp, making it a perfect habitat for fritillaries. They have a delicacy I adore, and a host of popular names, of which Chequered Lily is my own favorite. For this design I have paired the flowers, making the edging checked as well. It is a large piece of knitting, which can be ruined by uneven tension and by not twisting the wool properly across the back. The ribs, pocket edges, shoulder ruffles, and button bands are very strong, as they are all both Fair Isle and knitted double.

## MATERIALS

Pair of size 2 (2¼ mm) needles
Set of 4 double-pointed size 2 (2¼ mm) needles
2 pairs of size 3 (3¼ mm) needles
Circular size 3 (3¼ mm) needle 16 in (40 cm) long
8 stitch holders
7 buttons

## WEIGHT OF YARN AND COLORS

**Dark gray (A)**   18 oz (500 g)
**Natural (B)**   8 oz (230 g)
**Crimson (C)**   6 oz (170 g)
**Grass green (D)**   6 oz (170 g)

## MEASUREMENTS

Length from top of shoulder to bottom edge of jacket:
35 in (89 cm)
Actual width all around at underarm: 50 in (127 cm)
Sleeve length: 22½ in (57 cm)

## GAUGE

Over pattern, using size 3 (3¼ mm) needles (or size to
obtain gauge), 30 stitches and 30 rows to 4 in (10 cm).

## IMPORTANT

● Twist wools at back of work every 1–2 stitches to
avoid making holes, but do not pull tight.
● When working St st using just one color, twist a
spare ball of the same color yarn across the back of
work to keep the thickness of the garment even.
● When using the circular needle, loop a short strand
of brightly colored wool around the first stitch so that
you can find the beginning of each round easily.
● The sleeves are knitted from shoulder to wrist so the
panels must be worked in reverse order, that is, you
work from round 28 to 1.

# 64 FRITILLARY

CHART A
Top of garment

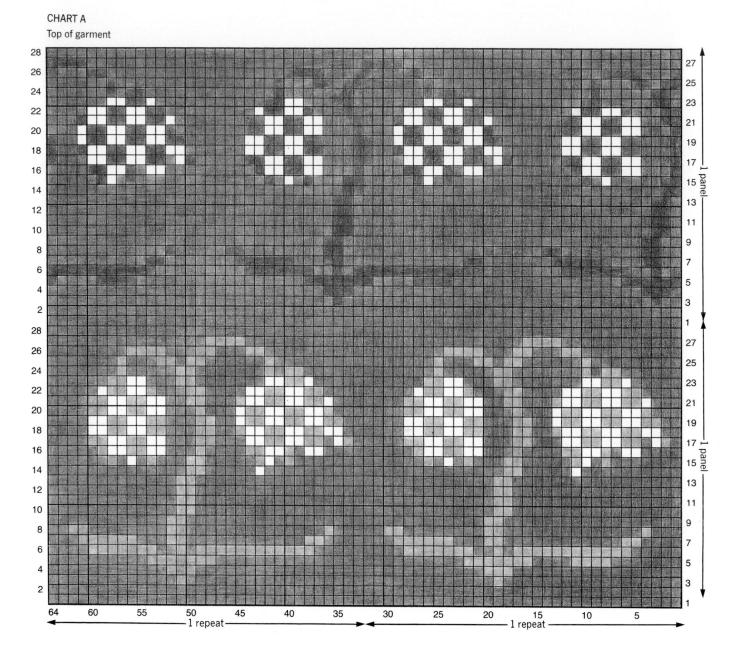

Bottom of garment

Odd-numbered rows are knit, worked from right to left.
Even-numbered rows are purl, worked from left to right.

CHART B

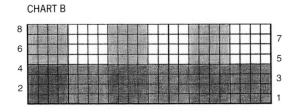

# INSTRUCTIONS
## FRONTS AND BACK

With size 2 (2¼ mm) needles and A, cast on 320 sts and work 32 rows from chart B.

**Next row** k in A.

**Next row** k in A (to make foldline), then beginning at st 1, row 5, work 32 more rows from chart B. Change to size 3 (3¼ mm) needles.

**Inc row** work row 1 of chart A in A and at the same time, k6, *k6, inc into next st; rep from * to last 6 sts, k6 (364 sts). Cont working from chart A until 2 panels have been worked.

## Pockets

Lay work aside and work Pocket linings. With size 3 (3¼ mm) needles and A, cast on 42 sts and work from chart A, beginning at st 29, row 1, until 2 complete panels have been worked. Keep sts on one of 2nd pair of size 3 (3¼ mm) needles. Rep for 2nd Pocket lining, beginning at st 7, row 1. Return to main body of work and cont as follows. Patt 28 sts, slip next 42 sts onto a st holder, then join on 1st Pocket lining, knitting from its needle, keeping to patt, and patt to last 70 sts. Slip next 42 sts onto a st holder, then join on 2nd Pocket lining, knitting from its needle, keeping to patt, and patt to end. Cont working from chart A until 5 panels and 14 rows have been worked from the beginning.

## Divide for fronts and back

With right side facing, patt 70 sts, turn. Cont on these sts until 7 panels and 6 rows have been worked from the beginning.

## Neck shaping

**Row 7** With right side facing, bind off 16 sts, patt to end (54 sts).

**Row 8** patt to last 3 sts, p2 tog, p1.

**Row 9** k1, k2 tog, patt to end (52 sts).

Rep the last 2 rows until 44 sts rem, then work straight until 8 panels from the beginning have been worked. Slip these 44 sts onto a st holder for right front shoulder. Return to rem 294 sts, slip next 42 sts onto a st holder for underarm, patt 140 sts, then turn. Work straight on these sts until 7 panels and 18 rows have been worked from the beginning.

**Row 19** patt 47 sts, k2 tog, k1, turn.

**Row 20** p1, p2 tog, patt to end.

**Row 21** patt to last 3 sts, k2 tog, k1.

Rep the last 2 rows until 44 sts rem, then work straight until 8 panels have been worked from the beginning. Slip sts onto a st holder for right back shoulder. With right side facing, slip next 40 sts onto a st holder for back neck, then work rem 50 sts as follows:

**Row 19** patt to end.

**Row 20** patt to last 3 sts, p2 tog, p1.

**Row 21** k1, k2 tog, patt to end.

Rep the last 2 rows until 44 sts rem, then work straight until 8 panels have been worked from the beginning. Slip sts onto a st holder for left back shoulder. With right

side facing, return to rem 112 sts, slip next 42 sts onto a st holder for underarm, then work straight on rem 70 sts until 7 panels and 7 rows have been worked from the beginning.

**Row 8** bind off 16 sts, patt to end (wrong side facing).

**Row 9** patt to last 3 sts, k2 tog, k1.

**Row 10** p1, p2 tog, patt to end.

Rep the last 2 rows until 44 sts rem, then work straight until 8 panels have been worked from the beginning. Leave sts on needles for left front shoulder.

## Shoulder seams

Block (see page 155) garment and press carefully on wrong side using a damp cloth. Graft (see page 155) right front shoulder to right back shoulder (right sides together). Rep for left shoulder.

## Finishing pockets

Slip the 42 sts on st holder on right front onto size 2 (2¼ mm) needle and beginning with st 1, row 5, and decreasing 2 sts across 1st row, work 12 rows from chart B.

**Rows 13 and 14** k in A (to make foldline).

**Rows 15–26** as chart B, then bind off loosely. Rep for left front, but begin with st 5, row 5. Fold pocket tops to inside along foldline and stitch down neatly. Stitch pocket linings in place carefully on wrong side. Fold welt to inside along foldline and stitch down neatly. Weave in any loose ends using a darning needle (do not just cut them off).

## SLEEVES

**Remember** all rounds are k and work chart A in rev order, from round 28–1.

With size 3 (3¼ mm) circular needle and A, slip the 42 sts from st holder onto needle and k in A, then pick up and k 118 sts around armhole (160 sts). Join. Work 5 complete panels as chart A.

Change to set of 4 double-pointed size 2 (2¼ mm) needles.

**Dec round 1** *k2 tog; rep from * to end (80 sts).

**Dec round 2** *k8, k2 tog; rep from * to end (72 sts). Work 40 rounds as chart B.

**Next round** k in A.

**Next round** p in A (to make foldline), then work 40 more rounds as chart B and bind off loosely. Rep for 2nd sleeve.

Weave in any loose ends using a darning needle and then block (see page 155) and press on wrong side using a damp cloth. Fold cuffs to inside along foldline and stitch down neatly.

## NECKBAND

With right side facing and size 2 (2¼ mm) needles and A, pick up and k 38 sts up right front to holder. K 40 sts from st holder, then pick up and k 38 sts down left front (116 sts).

**Row 1** p.

**Rows 2–13** as chart B, beginning at st 1, row 5, and

working 12 rows in patt.

**Rows 14 and 15** k in A (to make foldline).

**Rows 16–27** as chart B, then bind off loosely. Fold band to inside along foldline and stitch down neatly.

## BUTTONHOLE BAND

With right side facing and size 2 (2¼ mm) needles and A, pick up and k 192 sts up right front edge between but not including welt and neckband.

**Next row** p in A, then cut off A.

**Row 1** maintaining color sequence of checks on welt, pick up and k 32 sts up side of welt, patt the 192 sts, and then pick up and k 12 sts up edge of neckband (236 sts).

**Rows 2–5** work from chart B, then make buttonholes.

**Row 6** patt 4, *bind off 7, patt 30 (counting st already on needle); rep from * to last 10 sts, bind off 7, patt 3 (7 buttonholes).

**Row 7** patt, casting on 7 sts over the 7 buttonholes.

**Rows 8–12** work as chart B.

**Rows 13 and 14** k in A.

**Rows 15–19** work as chart B.

**Rows 20 and 21** as rows 6 and 7.

**Rows 22–26** work from chart B, then bind off loosely. Fold band to inside along foldline and stitch down neatly. Neaten around buttonhole using small buttonhole st.

## BUTTON BAND

With right side facing and size 2 (2¼ mm) needles and A, pick up and k 192 sts down left front edge between but not including neckband and welt.

**Next row** p in A, then cut off A.

**Row 1** maintaining color sequence of checks on neckband, pick up and k 12 sts down edge of neckband, patt the 192 sts, and then pick up and k 32 sts down side of welt (236 sts).

**Rows 2–12** work as chart B.

**Rows 13 and 14** k in A.

**Rows 15–26** work as chart B, then bind off loosely. Fold band to inside along foldline and stitch down neatly. Sew on buttons.

## ARMHOLE FRILL

With size 2 (2¼ mm) double-pointed needles and A, pick up and k 120 sts around top of right sleeve, beg at right back, but not including underarm, then work 2 rows in k1 p1 rib.

**Next row** inc into every st (240 sts). Work rows 5–8 from chart B. K next 2 rows in D (to make foldline), then repeat rows 5–8 as chart B. Bind off. Fold frill at foldline and slip st into place. Rep for other armhole, beg by picking up sts at left front.

# HARLEQUIN JACKET

Many painters have been drawn to the world of the music hall and circus, to the clown, pierrot, and acrobat. Picasso was particularly fond of the harlequin, whose sense of mischief and bespangled tights won Columbine's heart and made him so popular in pantomime. I have tried to echo that sense of theater in my design. The scarlets and yellows are bright and bold. Greens act as borders and divide the panels and checks. The collar, cuffs, and peplum add to its exuberance.

## MATERIALS
Pair of size 2 (2¼ mm) needles
Set of 4 double-pointed size 2 (2¼ mm) needles
Pair of size 3 (3¼ mm) needles
size G (3¼ mm) crochet hook
5 buttons

## WEIGHT OF YARN AND COLORS
Scarlet (A)    10 oz (280 g)
Blue-green (B)    8 oz (230 g)
Burgundy (C1)    2 oz (57 g)
Elderberry (C2)    2 oz (57 g)
Pale elderberry (C3)    2 oz (57 g)
Yellow (D1)    2 oz (57 g)
Buttercup yellow (D2)    2 oz (57 g)
Primrose (D3)    2 oz (57 g)

## MEASUREMENTS
Length from top of shoulder to top of peplum: 17½ in (44 cm)
Actual width all around at underarm: 44 in (112 cm)
Sleeve length (excluding frill): 18 in (46 cm)

CHART A

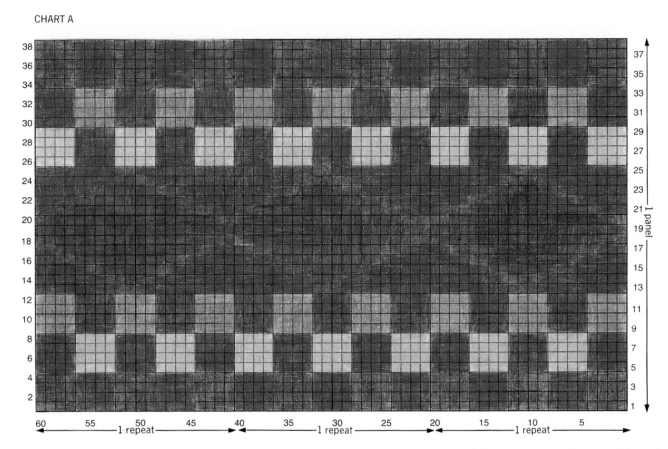

Odd-numbered rows are knit, worked from right to left.
Even-numbered rows are purl, worked from left to right.

## GAUGE

Over pattern, using size 3 (3¼ mm) needles (or size to obtain correct gauge), 26 sts and 30 rows to 4 in (10 cm).

## IMPORTANT

● Twist wools at back of work every 1–2 sts to avoid making holes, but do not pull tight.

● When working St st using just one color, twist a spare ball of the same color yarn across the back of work to keep the thickness of the garment even.

● Change shade of diamond motif every 2–3 rows to give a random effect.

● Work checks in one color at a time, but vary which color you use from panel to panel, especially for the collar, cuffs, and peplum.

● This garment is knitted sideways, beginning at the left front edge, and the sleeves are also knitted sideways.

● The fronts and back and sleeves are worked from 2 charts – A and B – alternately, so check that you are referring to the correct chart each time you start a new panel.

## INSTRUCTIONS
### FRONTS AND BACK
#### Panel 1

With size 3 (3¼ mm) needles and A, cast on 84 sts and work from chart A, beg at st 1, row 13, working diamonds in C1, 2, and 3 in random numbers of rows.

**Rows 13–20** as chart.

Cont working from chart, beg with right side row, inc alternate rows to shape neck as follows:

**Rows 21 and 23** patt to end, inc into last st.

**Rows 25 and 27** patt to end, cast on 2 sts.

**Rows 29 and 31** patt to end, cast on 3 sts.

**Rows 33 and 35** patt to end, cast on 5 sts (106 sts).

**Rows 36–38** as chart, then join on B and work 4 rows rev St st as follows.

**Row 1** k.

**Row 2** k.

**Row 3** p.

**Row 4** k.

#### Panel 2

Join on A and work from chart B, beg at st 1 row 1.

**Rows 1–37** as chart.

**Row 38** With wrong side facing bind off 52 sts (neck edge), patt to end (54 sts). Join on B and work 4 rows rev St st as before.

#### Panel 3 (underarm panel)

Join on A and work from chart A, beg at st 1, row 1.

**Rows 1–38** as chart. Join on B and work 4 rows rev St st as before.

#### Panel 4

Join on A and work from chart B, beg at st 1, row 1.

**Row 1** patt to end, cast on 52 sts (106 sts).

**Rows 2–38** as chart. Join on B and work 4 rows rev St st as before.

#### Panel 5

Join on A and work from chart A, beg at st 1, row 1.

**Rows 1–4** as chart.

**Rows 5–11** dec 1 st at end (neck edge) of next and following 3 alternate rows (102 sts).

**Rows 12–27** as chart.

CHART B

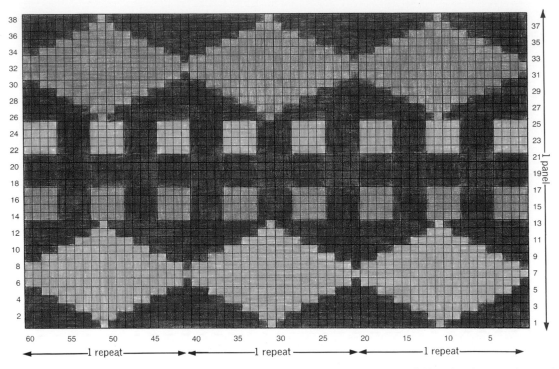

1 repeat — 1 repeat — 1 repeat

Odd-numbered rows are knit, worked from right to left.
Even-numbered rows are purl, worked from left to right.

**Rows 28–34** inc 1 st at beg (neck edge) of next and following 3 alternate rows (106 sts).
**Rows 35–38** as chart. Join on B and work 4 rows rev St st as before.

### Panel 6
Join on A and work from chart B, beg at st 1, row 1.
**Rows 1–37** as chart.
**Row 38** bind off 52 sts (neck edge), patt to end (54 sts). Join on B and work 4 rows rev St st as before.

### Panel 7 (underarm panel)
Join on A and work from chart A, beg at st 1, row 1.
**Rows 1–38** as chart. Join on B and work 4 rows rev St st as before.

### Panel 8
Join on A and work from chart B, beg at st 1, row 1.
**Row 1** patt to end, cast on 52 sts (106 sts).
**Rows 2–38** as chart. Join on B and work 4 rows rev St st as before.

### Panel 9
Join on A and work from chart A, beg at st 1, row 1.
**Rows 1–3** as chart.
Cont working from chart, dec alternate rows as follows:
**Rows 4 and 6** bind off 5 sts (neck edge), patt to end.
**Rows 8 and 10** bind off 3 sts (neck edge), patt to end.
**Rows 12 and 14** bind off 2 sts (neck edge), patt to end.

**Rows 16 and 18** bind off 1 st (neck edge), patt to end (84 sts).
**Rows 19–25** as chart.
**Row 26** p using A only, then bind off loosely in A. Weave in any loose ends using a darning needle (do not just cut them off). Block (see page 155) garment and press carefully on wrong side using a damp cloth.

### Shoulder seams
With right side facing and size 2 (2¼mm) needles and B, pick up and k 40 sts along right front shoulder and work 4 rows rev St st as follows:
**Row 1** k.
**Row 2** p.
**Row 3** k.
**Row 4** p. Leave sts on a spare needle for grafting.
With right side facing and size 2 (2¼ mm) needles and B, pick up and k 40 sts along right back shoulder. Leave sts on needle. Graft (see page 155) right front shoulder to right back shoulder (right sides together). Rep for left shoulder.

### SLEEVES
With size 3 (3¼ mm) needles and A, cast on 111 sts. Work 6 complete panels from charts in order A, B, A, B, A and B. Work 4 rows rev St st in B between each panel and end with 4 rows rev St st in B. Leave sts on needle. Press carefully on wrong side using a damp cloth. Graft (see page 155) sts on needle to sts of cast-on edge

(right sides together). Weave in any loose ends using a darning needle (do not cut off). Rep for 2nd sleeve.

### Cuffs
With right side facing, making sure patt is right way up, and a set of 4 double-pointed size 2 (2¼ mm) needles and B, pick up and k 160 sts along lower edge of sleeve.
**Round 1** *p2 tog; rep from * to end (80 sts).
**Round 2** *p2, p2 tog; rep from * to end (60 sts).
**Round 3** p.
**Round 4** k.
**Rounds 5–7** p.
**Round 8** k.
**Rounds 9–11** p.
**Round 12** k.
**Rounds 13–15** p.
**Round 16** k, then bind off loosely.
**Frill** With size 3 (3¼ mm) needles and B, cast on 20 sts and k 2 rows. Join on A and work from chart C, shaping as follows:
**Row 1** k.
**Row 2** p 19 sts, turn.
**Row 3** k.
**Row 4** p 18 sts, turn.
**Row 5** k.
**Row 6** p 17 sts, turn.
**Row 7** k to end.
**Row 8** p to end.

**Rows 9 and 10** join on B and k across all sts.
Rep these 10 rows as chart C until 16 panels have been worked, ending panel 16 with row 8. Keep sts on needle. Then, graft (see page 155) sts on needle to cast-on edge (right sides tog).
With set of 4 double-pointed size 2 (2¼ mm) needles and B, pick up and k 120 sts along shaped edge of Frill.
**Dec round** *k2 tog; rep from * to end (60 sts), then bind off loosely.
Stitch this edge of Frill to cast off edge of Cuff using small back sts (right sides tog). Rep for 2nd sleeve.

## WELT

With right side facing and size 2 (2¼ mm) needles and B, pick up and k 170 sts along lower edge of fronts and back.
**Row 1** k.
**Row 2** p.
**Rows 3–5** k.
**Row 6** p
**Rows 7 and 8** k.
Rep rows 1–8 once and keep sts on needle.

## PEPLUM

With size 3 (3¼ mm) needles and A, cast on 36 sts and work from chart C, shaping as follows:
**Row 1** k.
**Row 2** p 35 sts, turn.
**Row 3** k.
**Row 4** p 34 sts, turn.
**Row 5** k.
**Row 6** p 33 sts, turn.
**Row 7** k to end.
**Row 8** p to end.

**Rows 9 and 10** join on B and k across all sts.
Rep these 10 rows as chart C until 57 panels have been worked, ending panel 57 with row 8, then bind off loosely.
With right side facing and size 2 (2¼ mm) needles and B, pick up and k 340 sts along shaped edge of Peplum.
**Dec row** *k2 tog; rep from * to end (170 sts). Keep sts on needle and graft (see page 155) them to sts on needle for Welt (right sides tog).

## NECKBAND

With wrong side facing and size 2 (2¼ mm) needles and B, pick up and k 87 sts along neck edge, beg at left front edge. Work 4 rows rev St st as follows:
**Row 1** k.
**Row 2** p.
**Row 3** k.
**Row 4** p. Leave sts on needle.

## COLLAR

With size 3 (3¼ mm) needles and A, cast on 28 sts and work from chart C, shaping as follows:
**Row 1** k.
**Row 2** p 27 sts, turn.
**Row 3** k.
**Row 4** p 26 sts, turn.
**Row 5** k.
**Row 6** p 25 sts, turn.
**Row 7** k.
**Row 8** p.
**Rows 9 and 10** join on B and k.
Rep these 10 rows as chart C until 29 panels have been worked, ending panel 29 with row 8, then bind off loosely.

With right side facing and size 2 (2¼ mm) needles and B, pick up and k 174 sts along shaped edge of Collar.
**Dec row** *k2 tog; rep from * to end (87 sts). Keep sts on needle and graft (see page 155) them to sts of Neckband.

## BUTTONHOLE BAND

With right side facing and size 2 (2¼ mm) needles and B, pick up and k 100 sts up right front edge, beg at lower edge of Welt.
**Row 1** k.
**Row 2** p.
**Rows 3–5** k, then make buttonholes.
**Row 6** p3, bind off 6 sts, *p16 (including st on right-hand needle), bind off 6; rep from * to last 3 sts, p3.
**Row 7** k, casting on 6 sts over the 5 buttonholes.
**Rows 8 and 9** k.
**Row 10** p.
**Rows 11–13** k.
**Row 14** p.
**Rows 15–17** k.
**Rows 18 and 19** as rows 6 and 7.
**Rows 20 and 21** k.
**Row 22** p.
**Row 23** k, then bind off loosely purlwise.
Fold band to inside and stitch down neatly, neatening around buttonholes using a small buttonhole st.

## BUTTON BAND

With right side facing and size 2 (2¼ mm) needles and B, pick and k 100 sts down left front edge to lower edge of Welt. K 1 row, p 1 row, k 3 rows, p 1 row, k 3 rows, p 1 row, k 3 rows, p 1 row, k 3 rows, p 1 row, k 3 rows, p 1 row, k 1 row, then bind off loosely purlwise. Fold band to inside and stitch down neatly. Sew on buttons.

## SLEEVE INSERTION

Make 4 pleats – 2 each side of center panel, 2 facing front and 2 facing back – as follows. With panel 4 as center panel, take left-hand edge of panel 4 – folding along left-hand edge of rev St st – to center of panel 3 and take left-hand edge of panel 3 – also folding along left-hand edge of rev St st – to center of panel 2, then take right-hand edge of panel 4 – folding along right-hand edge of rev St st – to center of panel 5 and take right-hand edge of panel 5 – also folding along right-hand edge of rev St st – to center of panel 6. Stitch pleats down neatly.
With right side facing and a set of 4 double-pointed size 2 (2¼ mm) needles and B, pick up and k 132 sts along top edge of sleeve. Work 4 rounds in p and keep sts on needles.
Place sleeve in armhole (right sides tog) and match panel 1 with underarm panel of fronts and back and center of panel 4 with shoulder seam. Graft (see page 155) sts of sleeve to sts of armhole. Rep for 2nd sleeve.
With size G (3¼ mm) crochet hook and B, work 2 rows single crochet (see page 155) along edges of Collar, Cuff frills, and Peplum.

CHART C

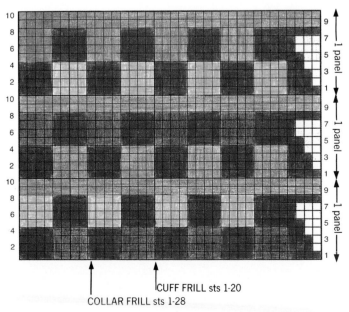

1 panel
1 panel
1 panel
1 panel

CUFF FRILL sts 1-20
COLLAR FRILL sts 1-28

# PATCHWORK FANS CARDIGAN

Two of my knitters are sisters in their seventies who both adore knitting. They laugh a lot as well, which makes visiting them a delight. One knits the most perfect Fair Isle cardigans I have ever seen, but the other can only knit plain sweaters. This design was the result of trying to create something specially for her. The knitting has a patchwork effect and the fans are knitted separately and appliquéd on afterward, using the traditional Dorset feather stitch. The dyeing is made quicker if all the navy is done in one go, and the fans can be in any color combination you like. It's a good sweater for using up leftover yarn.

## MATERIALS

Pair of size 2 (2¼ mm) needles
Set of 4 double-pointed size 2 (2¼ mm) needles
Pair of size 3 (3¼ mm) needles
Circular size 3 (3¼ mm) needles 16 in (40 cm) long
6 stitch holders
6 buttons

## WEIGHT OF YARN AND COLORS

**Navy (A)**    16 oz (460 g)
**Natural (B)**    3 oz (85 g)
**Red (C)**    3 oz (85 g)
**Dark indigo blue (D)**    3 oz (85 g)

## MEASUREMENTS

Length from top of shoulder to bottom edge of cardigan: 21 in (53.5 cm)
Actual width all around at underarm: 48 in (122 cm)
Sleeve length: 20 in (51 cm)

## GAUGE

Over double moss stitch, using size 3 (3¼ mm) needles (or size to obtain gauge), 26 stitches and 32 rows to 4 in (10 cm).

## IMPORTANT

- The fans are knitted separately and appliquéed on.
- The sleeves are knitted from shoulder to cuff.
- As the sleeves are worked on circular needles all stitches are knit unless otherwise stated.

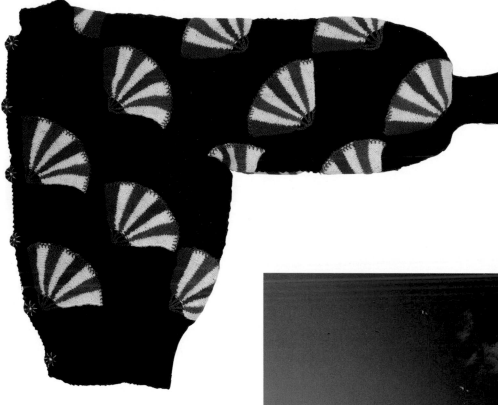

## INSTRUCTIONS
### FRONTS AND BACK

With size 2 (2¼ mm) needles and A, cast on 280 sts and work 43 rows in k1 p1 rib.

**Inc row** *rib 13, inc into next st; rep from * to end (300 sts). Change to size 3 (3¼ mm) needles and patt (right side facing) as follows:

**Row 1** *[k2 p2] 7 times, k2, p30; rep from * to end.
**Row 2** *k30, [p2 k2] 7 times, p2; rep from * to end.
**Row 3** *[p2 k2] 7 times, p2, p30; rep from * to end.
**Row 4** *k30, [p2 k2] 7 times, k2; rep from * to end.
**Rows 5–34** rep these 4 rows 7 times then rows 1–2 once.
**Row 35** *p30, [k2 p2] 7 times, k2; rep from * to end.
**Row 36** *[p2 k2] 7 times, p2, k30; rep from * to end.
**Row 37** *p30, [p2 k2] 7 times, p2; rep from * to end.
**Row 38** *[k2 p2] 7 times, k2, k30; rep from * to end.
**Rows 39–68** rep rows 35–38 7 times and then rows 35–36 once.

These 68 rows form patt.
Cont in patt, working rows 1–20 again.

### Divide for fronts and back

**Row 21** With right side facing patt 56 sts, turn and leave rem sts on a spare needle. Cont in patt on these 56 sts for right front until row 68 has been worked, ending at front edge.

### Neck shaping

**Row 1** With right side facing bind off 12 sts, patt to end.
**Rows 2–9** cont in patt, dec 1 st at neck edge every row (36 sts).
**Rows 10–16** work in patt, then slip sts onto a st holder for shoulder grafting.
Return to rem 244 sts on spare needle. With right side facing slip next 38 sts onto a st holder for right underarm and patt 112 sts (row 21), turn.
**Row 22** cont in patt on these 112 sts until row 68 has been worked. Then work rows 1–12 of patt.
**Rows 13–16** With right side facing patt 38 sts, k2 tog, turn, then dec 1 st at this edge (neck edge) on next 3 rows (36 sts).
**Row 17** patt, then slip sts onto a st holder for shoulder grafting. Slip next 32 sts onto a st holder for back neck, then return to rem 40 sts, k2 tog, then patt (row 13) to end (39 sts).
**Row 14** patt to last 2 sts, k2 tog (neck edge).
**Rows 15 and 16** dec 1 st at neck edge (36 sts).
**Row 17** patt, then slip sts onto a st holder for shoulder grafting. Return to rem 94 sts and with right side facing slip next 38 sts onto a st holder for left underarm, then patt to end (56 sts). Cont in patt until row 68 has been worked.
**Row 1** With right side facing patt to end.
**Row 2** With wrong side facing bind off 12 sts, patt to end.
**Rows 3–10** dec 1 st at neck edge every row (36 sts).
**Rows 11–16** patt, then leave sts on needle for shoulder.

### SHOULDER SEAMS

Graft (see page 155) right front shoulder to right back shoulder (right sides together). Rep for left shoulder.

### SLEEVES

With right side facing and size 3 (3¼ mm) circular needle, work 38 sts on st holder for first armhole as follows: k3, *k2 tog, k2; rep from * to last 3 sts, k3 (30 sts). Then pick up and k 90 sts around armhole (120 sts). For right sleeve, beg at round 1 of patt (m st) and for left sleeve, beg at round 35 of patt (rev St st) as sleeve and body patches at underarm and patches at shoulder will then match.

Work 136 rounds in patt as below:
**Rounds 1–2** *[k2, p2] 7 times, k2, p30; rep from * around.
**Rounds 3–4** *[p2, k2] 7 times, p2, p30; rep from * around.
**Rounds 5–34** Rep these 4 rounds 7 times and rounds 1–2 again.
**Rounds 35–36** *p30, [k2, p2] 7 times, k2; rep from * around.
**Rounds 37–38** *p30, [p2, k2] 7 times, p2; rep from * around.
**Rounds 39–68** Rep rounds 35–38 7 times and rounds 35–36 again.

Change to set of 4 double-pointed size 2 (2¼ mm) needles.
**Dec round 1** *p2, p2 tog; rep from * around (90 sts).
**Dec round 2** *p1, p2 tog; rep from * around (60 sts).

### Cuffs

Work 45 rounds in k1 p1 rib. Join on 2nd strand and using yarn double bind off loosely in rib. Weave in any loose ends using a darning needle (do not just cut them off). Block (see page 155) garment and press carefully on wrong side using a damp cloth, but do not press ribbing.

### NECKBAND

With right side facing and size 2 (2¼ mm) needles, pick up and k 39 sts from right front neck edge to st holder. Then k 32 sts from st holder and pick up and k 39 sts to left front neck edge (110 sts). Work 9 rows in k1 p1 rib. Next row p (to make foldline), then work 9 more rows in k1 p1 rib. Bind off loosely in rib. Fold band to inside along foldline and stitch down neatly.

### BUTTONHOLE BAND

With right side facing and size 2 (2¼ mm) needles, pick up and k 162 sts up right front edge.
**Rows 1–4** work in k1 p1 rib, then make buttonholes:
**Row 5** rib 3, bind off 6 sts, *rib 24 (counting st already on needle), bind off 6 sts; rep from * to last 3 sts, rib 3.
**Row 6** cont in k1 p1 rib, casting on 6 sts over the 6 buttonholes.
**Rows 7–9** work in k1 p1 rib.
**Row 10** p (to make foldline).
**Rows 11–13** work in k1 p1 rib.

**Rows 14 and 15** as rows 5 and 6.
**Rows 16–19** work in k1 p1 rib, then bind off loosely in rib. Fold band to inside along foldline and stitch down neatly, neatening around buttonholes using a small buttonhole st.

### BUTTON BAND

With right side facing and size 2 (2¼ mm) needles, pick up and k 162 sts down left front edge. Work 9 rows in k1 p1 rib, p next row (to make foldline), work 9 more rows in k1 p1 rib, then bind off loosely in rib. Fold band to inside along foldline and stitch down. Sew on buttons.

### FANS

With size 2 (2¼ mm) needles and C, cast on 22 sts.
**Row 1** k.
**Row 2** p19, turn.
**Row 3** k.
**Row 4** p12, turn.
**Row 5** k.
**Row 6** p5, turn.
**Row 7** k.
**Row 8** p21, slip 1.

**Rows 1–8** form one section of fan. Rep rows 1–8 7 more times, making 7 more sections using colors in following order: B, D, B, C, B, D, B, then bind off. Make 35 more fans. Place a fan in each rev St st square, all facing the same way. With a darning needle and strand of B, slip st bottom of fan into place using small, neat sts. With strand of C, sew vertical edge of fan into place. With strand of D, feather st top edge of fan (see below). With strand of D, sew 5 small rows of chain st (see page 157) from bottom edge of fan into corner of rev St st square (see picture). Rep for each fan.

### FEATHER STITCH

This is worked from top to bottom. Bring the needle up through the work, where you want the centerline of the stitches to be. Insert the needle at a point slightly lower and to the left, and slant it to the right, so that you can bring it out on the centerline with the thread looped *under* the point of the needle. Next insert the needle slightly lower and to the right this time and, slanting it to the left, make a similar looped stitch. Continue, alternating the stitches from left to right, keeping them evenly spaced.

# BELLS AND CHECKS CARDIGAN

I have always loved the attention to detail in Elizabethan costume – the way bows, pleating and embroidery transformed a commonplace garment into something out of the ordinary. On this jacket every panel has a different color and pattern combination, and the pleated sleeves are deliberately grafted onto the body so they don't match, making it random and theatrical. Weave the wool on every stitch and pay as much attention to the inside of the jacket as the outside.

## MATERIALS
Pair of size 2 (2¼ mm) needles
Set of 4 double-pointed size 2 (2¼ mm) needles
Pair of size 3 (3¼ mm) needles
7 buttons

## WEIGHT OF YARN AND COLORS
**Dark indigo blue (A)**   8 oz (230 g)
**Crimson (B)**   10 oz (280 g)
**Navy (C)**   12 oz (340 g)
**Natural (D)**   6 oz (170 g)

## MEASUREMENTS
Length from top of shoulder to bottom edge of cardigan: 24 in (61 cm)
Actual width all around at underarm: 58 in (147 cm)
Sleeve length: 20 in (51 cm)

## GAUGE
Over pattern, using size 3 (3¼ mm) needles (or size to obtain gauge), 30 stitches and 30 rows to 10 cm (4 in).

## IMPORTANT

● Twist wools at back of work every 1–2 stitches to avoid making holes, but do not pull tight.

● When working St st using just one color, twist a spare ball of the same color yarn across the back of work to keep the thickness of the garment even.

● This garment is knitted sideways, beginning at the left front edge, and the sleeves are also knitted sideways.

● Before beginning each new panel, check with the diagram below to ensure that you have the correct color combination.

Key

S = background A, flower B, stem C
T = checks in B and D
U = background B, flower C, stem D
V = checks in B and C
W = background C, flower D, stem B
X = checks in A and D
Y = checks in A and B
Z = checks in C and D

## INSTRUCTIONS
## FRONTS AND BACK

### Panel 1

With size 3 (3¼ mm) needles and color combination S, cast on 126 sts in A and work from chart A, beginning at st 1, row 1.

**Rows 1–12** as chart.

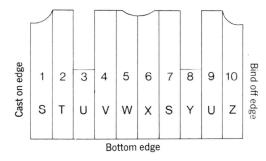

Bottom edge

### Neck shaping

**Row 13** With right side facing inc 1 st at end (neck edge) of row.

**Rows 14–16** as chart.

**Rows 17–29** inc 1 st at end (neck edge) of this and next 6 alternate rows (134 sts).

**Rows 30–31** as chart.

**Row 32** With wrong side facing cast on 15 sts (neck edge), patt to end (149 sts).

**Rows 33–42** as chart, then work 4 rows rev St st in C as follows:

**Row 1** k.

**Row 2** k.

**Row 3** p.

**Row 4** k.

### Panel 2

Using color combination T, work from chart B, beginning at st 1, row 1.

**Rows 1–41** as chart.

**Row 42** With wrong side facing bind off 52 sts (neck edge), patt to end (97 sts). Then join on C and work 4 rows rev St st as before.

CHART A

Odd-numbered rows are knit, worked from right to left.
Even-numbered rows are purl, worked from left to right.

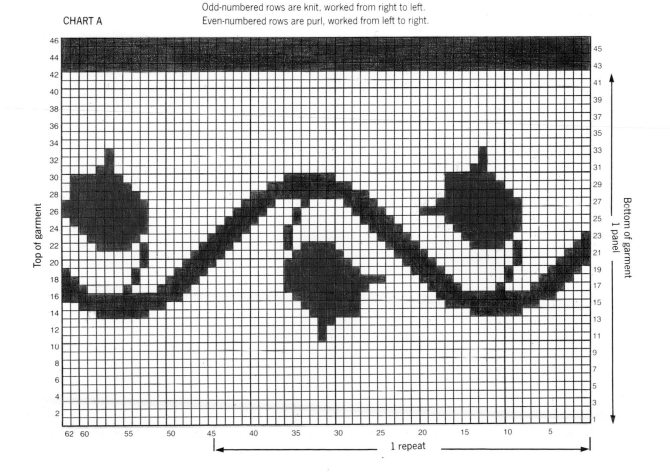

1 repeat

CHART B

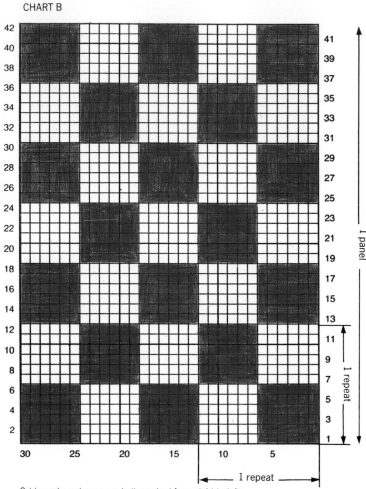

Odd-numbered rows are knit, worked from right to left.
Even-numbered rows are purl, worked from left to right.

**Panel 3** (underarm panel)
Using color combination U, work from chart A.
Rows 1–42 as chart, then work 4 rows rev St st in C as before.

**Panel 4**
Using color combination V, work from chart B.
Row 1 With right side facing patt to end of row (neck edge) then cast on 52 sts (149 sts).
Rows 2–42 as chart, then work 4 rows rev St st in C as before.

**Panel 5**
Using color combination W, work from chart A.
Rows 1–10 as chart.
Rows 11–15 dec 1 st at end (neck edge) of this and next 2 alternate rows (146 sts).
Rows 16–42 as chart, then work 4 rows rev St st in C as before.

**Panel 6**
Using color combination X, work from chart B.
Rows 1–26 as chart.

Rows 27–31 inc 1 st at end (neck edge) of this and next 2 alternate rows (149 sts).
Rows 32–42 as chart, then join on C and work 4 rows rev St st as before.

**Panel 7**
Using color combination S, work from chart A
Rows 1–41 as chart.
Row 42 With wrong side facing bind off 52 sts (neck edge), patt to end (97 sts), then work 4 rows rev St st in C as before.

**Panel 8** (underarm panel)
Using color combination Y, work from chart B.
Rows 1–42 as chart, then join on C and work 4 rows rev St st as before.

**Panel 9**
Using color combination U, work from chart A.
Row 1 With right side facing patt to end of row (neck edge), then cast on 52 sts (149 sts).
Rows 2–42 as chart, then work 4 rows rev St st in C as before.

**Panel 10**
Using color combination Z, work from chart B.
Rows 1–11 as chart.
Neck shaping
Row 12 With wrong side facing bind off 15 sts, patt to end (134 sts).
Rows 13–14 as chart.
Rows 15–27 dec 1 st at end (neck edge) of this and next 6 alternate rows (127 sts).
Rows 28–30 as chart.
Row 31 dec 1 st at end (neck edge) of row (126 sts).
Rows 32–42 as chart, then bind off loosely. Weave in any loose ends with a darning needle (do not just cut them off). Block (see page 155) garment and press carefully on wrong side using a damp cloth.

**Shoulder seams**
With right side facing and size 2 (2¼ mm) needles and C, pick up and k 52 sts along right front shoulder. K 1 row, p 1 row and k 1 row. Leave sts on a spare needle for grafting.
With size 2 (2¼ mm) needles and C, pick up and k 52 sts along right back shoulder and leave sts on needle for grafting. Graft (see page 155) right front shoulder to right back shoulder (right sides tog). Rep for left shoulder.

**SLEEVES**
**Left sleeve**
With size 3 (3¼ mm) needles and A, cast on 123 sts. Work 6 complete panels with 4 rows rev st st in C between each panel with color combinations in following order:
Panel 1 (underarm panel) Y.
Panel 2 U.
Panel 3 Z.
Panel 4 W.
Panel 5 X.
Panel 6 S.
Then work 4 rows rev St st in C and keep sts on needle. Weave in any loose ends using a darning needle (do not just cut them off). Press carefully on wrong side using a damp cloth, then graft (see page 155) sts on needle to cast on edge (right sides tog).

**Right sleeve**
Work as left sleeve but in following color combinations:
Panel 1 (underarm panel) W.
Panel 2 X.
Panel 3 S.
Panel 4 T.
Panel 5 U.
Panel 6 V.

## Cuffs

With set of 4 double-pointed size 2 (2¼ mm) needles and C, pick up and k 160 sts around lower edge of sleeve (making sure patt is right way up and right side is facing). Loop a short strand of brightly colored wool around 1st st of each round so that you can find beg of round easily.

**Round 1** *k2 tog; rep from * to end (80 sts).
**Round 2** *k2, k2 tog; rep from * to end (60 sts).
Join on 2nd strand C and using yarn double work 32 rounds in k1 p1 rib, then bind off loosely in rib.

## WELT

With right side facing and size 2 (2¼ mm) needles and C, pick up and k 230 sts along lower edge of fronts and back. Join on 2nd strand C and using yarn double work 32 rows in k1 p1 rib. Bind off loosely in rib.

## NECKBAND

With right side facing and size 2 (2¼ mm) needles and C, pick up and k 100 sts around neck, beg at right front neck edge. Join on 2nd strand C and using yarn double work 9 rows in k1 p1 rib, then bind off loosely in rib.

## BUTTONHOLE BAND

With right side facing and size 2 (2¼ mm) needles and C, pick up and k 152 sts up right front edge.
**Rows 1–4** join on 2nd strand C and using yarn double work in k1 p1 rib, then make buttonholes.
**Row 5** rib 4, *bind off 6 sts, rib 17 (counting st on needle); rep from * to last 10 sts, bind off 6 sts, rib 4.
**Row 6** work in k1 p1 rib, casting on 6 sts over the 7 buttonholes.
**Rows 7 and 8** work in k1 p1 rib, then bind off loosely in rib.

## BUTTON BAND

With right side facing and size 2 (2¼ mm) needles and C, pick up and k 152 sts down left front edge. Join on 2nd strand C and using yarn double work 8 rows in k1 p1 rib, then bind off loosely in rib. Sew on buttons.

## SLEEVE INSERTION

Make 3 pleats in top of sleeve by folding rev St st edge of panel 4 to centre of panel 3, rev St st edge of panel 5 to center of panel 4 and rev St st edge of panel 6 to centre of panel 5. Stitch the pleats down neatly (check that pleats face front of garment).
With set of 4 double-pointed size 2 (2¼ mm) needles and C, pick up and k 110 sts around top edge of sleeve (right side facing) and p 3 rounds. Leave sts on needle. Place sleeve in armhole (right sides tog), matching underarm panel and middle pleat with shoulder seam, and graft (see page 155) tog. Weave in any rem loose ends using a darning needle (do not just cut them off).

# CHEVRON JACKET

A few years ago my work was exhibited in Japan, which meant going out there to talk about it. I slipped away whenever I could, walking endlessly down narrow back streets in search of kimonos made out of naturally dyed fabric. Sadly, the ancient traditions of natural dyeing are virtually extinct, and the nearest I came to success was a tiny shop in Kyoto piled high with scraps of fabric. The old man who ran it spoke no English, and my Japanese is nonexistent. Yet our love of textiles overcame the language barrier, and I eventually left with a small length of chevron-patterned kimono fabric – the origin of this design. The triangles, squares, and circles are geometric like the chevron, yet act as a contrast and foil. The box-pleated sleeves and center back box pleat make the rest of the coat as much of a surprise as the front. Knit the variegated red colours randomly, and do the same with the elderberries.

## MATERIALS

Pair of size 2 (2¼ mm) needles
2 pairs of size 3 (3¼ mm) needles
Circular size 3 (3¼ mm) needle 16 in (40 cm) long
Set of 4 double-pointed size 3 (3¼ mm) needles
Size 3 (3¼ mm) cable needle
2 stitch holders
7 buttons

## WEIGHT OF YARN AND COLORS

Navy (A)    16 oz (450 g)
Natural (B)    8 oz (230 g)
Blue-green (C)    8 oz (230 g)
Scarlet (D1)    2 oz (57 g)
Crimson (D2)    2 oz (57 g)
Red (D3)    2 oz (57 g)
Medium indigo blue (E)    8 oz (230 g)
Elderberry (F1)    2 oz (57 g)
Light elderberry (F2)    2 oz (57 g)
Grape (F3)    2 oz (57 g)

## MEASUREMENTS

Length from top of shoulder to bottom edge of coat:
35½ in (90 cm)
Actual width all around at underarm: 49 in (124 cm)
Sleeve length: 19 in (48 cm)

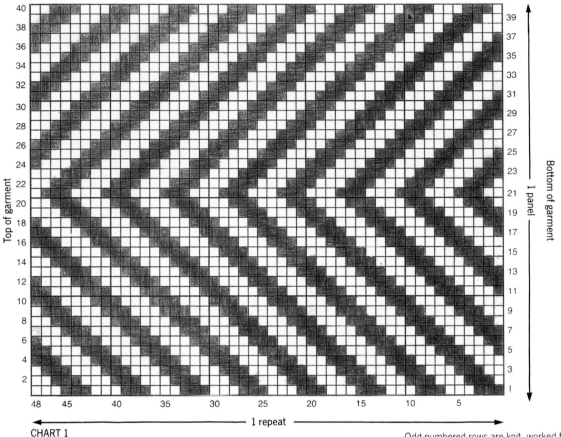

40 38 36 34 32 30 28 26 24 22 20 18 16 14 12 10 8 6 4 2

Top of garment

48 45 40 35 30 25 20 15 10 5

CHART 1

Bottom of garment
1 panel

39 37 35 33 31 29 27 25 23 21 19 17 15 13 11 9 7 5 3 1

1 repeat

Odd-numbered rows are knit, worked from right to left.
Even-numbered rows are purl, worked from left to right.

## GAUGE
Over pattern, using size 3 (3¼ mm) needles (or size to obtain gauge), 31 stitches and 30 rows to 4 in (10 cm).

## IMPORTANT
- Twist wools at back of work every 1–2 stitches to avoid making holes, but do not pull tight.
- When working St st using just one color, twist a spare ball of the same color yarn across the back of work to keep the thickness of the garment even.
- This garment is knitted sideways, beginning at the left front edge, and the sleeves are also knitted sideways.
- When using the circular needle, all rounds are knit.
- Change colors of shapes motifs every 2–3 rows to give a random effect.
- Chart 2 is worked in different color combinations, so before beginning each new panel, check that you have the correct color combination: for the fronts and back, panels 2, 6 and 10 are in background color C and the motif is in shades of D, panels 4 and 8 are in background color E and the motif is in shades of F; for the sleeves, panels 2 and 6 are in background color E and the motif is in F and panel 4 is in background color C and the motif is in D.
- When working sleeves, begin chart 1 at stitch 1, row 1, and chart 2 at sitch 26, row 1.

## INSTRUCTIONS
### FRONTS AND BACK
#### Panel 1
With size 3 (3¼ mm) needles and A, cast on 200 sts. Join on B and work from chart 1, beg at st 1, row 21.
**Rows 1–6** (rows 21–26 of chart) as chart.
Cont working from chart, inc alternate rows as follows:
**Row 7** With right side facing, patt to end, then cast on 2 sts (neck edge).
**Row 9** patt to end, cast on 2 sts (neck edge).
**Row 11** patt to end, cast on 3 sts (neck edge).
**Row 13** patt to end, cast on 3 sts (neck edge).
**Row 15** patt to end, cast on 5 sts (neck edge).
**Row 17** patt to end, cast on 5 sts (neck edge).
**Row 19** patt to end, cast on 5 sts (neck edge; 225 sts).
**Row 20** as chart, then join on 2nd strand A and work cable panel as follows:
**Row 1** *k3, slip next 3 sts onto cable needle and leave at front of work, k 3 sts, then k 3 sts from cable needle; rep from * to end.
**Rows 2–6** work in St st.
**Row 7** as row 1.
**Row 8** p.

#### Panel 2
Join on C and D and work from chart 2, beg at st 1, row 1.

**Rows 1–31** as chart.
**Pocket lining** Lay work aside and with 2nd pair of size 3 (3¼ mm) needles and C and D, cast on 60 sts and work rows 1–31 of chart 2, beg at st 30, row 1. Keep sts on spare needle.
Return to main body of work and cont as follows:
**Row 32** With wrong side facing, bind off 56 sts, patt 80 (including st on needle). Slip next 46 sts onto a st holder, then join on Pocket lining, p first 46 sts from its needle, then purl together last 14 sts of Pocket lining and next 14 sts of left front and patt to end (169 sts). Then join on 2 strands A and work 8 rows of cable panel in A as before.

#### Panel 3 (underarm panel)
Join on B and work from chart 1, beg at st 1, row 1.
**Rows 1–40** as chart, then join on 2nd strand A and work 8 rows of cable panel in A as before.

#### Panel 4
Join on E and F and work from chart 2, beg at st 1, row 1.
**Row 1** With right side facing, patt to end (neck edge) then cast on 56 sts (225 sts).
**Rows 2–32** as chart, then join on 2 strands A and work 8 rows of cable panel as before.

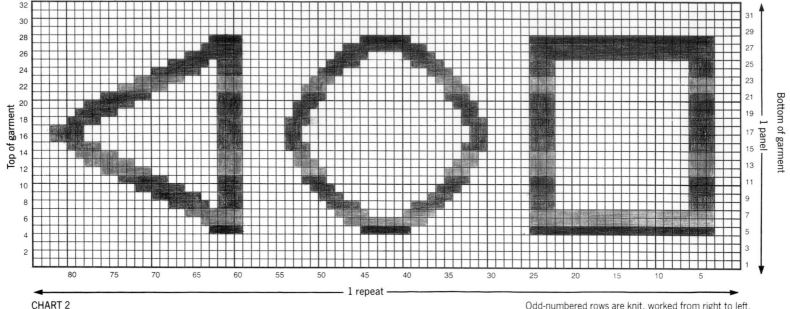

CHART 2

1 repeat

Odd-numbered rows are knit, worked from right to left.
Even-numbered rows are purl, worked from left to right.

### Panel 5
Join on B and work from chart 1, beg at st 1, row 1.
**Rows 1–40** as chart, then join on 2nd strand A and work 8 rows of cable panel as before.

### Panel 6
Join on C and D and work from chart 2, beg at st 1, row 1.
**Rows 1–32** as chart, then join on 2 strands A and work 8 rows of cable panel as before.

### Panel 7
Join on B and work from chart 1, beg at st 1, row 1.
**Rows 1–40** as chart, then join on 2nd strand A and work 8 rows of cable panel as before.

### Panel 8
Join on E and F and work from chart 2, beg at st 1, row 1.
**Rows 1–31** as chart.
**Row 32** With wrong side facing, bind off 56 sts, patt to end (169 sts), then join on 2 strands A and work 8 rows of cable panel as before.

### Panel 9 (underarm panel)
Join on B and work from chart 1, beg at st 1, row 1.
**Rows 1–40** as chart, then join on 2nd strand A and work 8 rows of cable panel as before.
**Pocket top** Lay work aside and, with size 3 (3¼ mm) needles and 2 strands A, cast on 46 sts and work 8 rows of cable panel as before. Keep sts on spare needle. Return to main body of work and cont as follows:

### Panel 10
Join on C and D and work from chart 2, beg at st 1, row 1.
**Row 1** With wrong side facing, patt 43 sts, slip sts of Pocket top onto needle and k them. Slip next 46 sts onto a st holder, patt 80 sts, then turn and cast on 56 sts (225 sts).
**Rows 2–32** as chart, then join on 2 strands A and work 8 rows of cable panel as before.

### Panel 11
Join on B and work from chart 1, beg at st 1, row 1, dec alternate rows as follows:
**Row 2** With wrong side facing, bind off 5 sts, patt to end.
**Row 4** bind off 5 sts (neck edge), patt to end.
**Row 6** bind off 5 sts (neck edge), patt to end.
**Row 8** bind off 3 sts (neck edge), patt to end.
**Row 10** bind off 3 sts (neck edge), patt to end.
**Row 12** bind off 2 sts (neck edge), patt to end.
**Row 14** bind off 2 sts (neck edge), patt to end (200 sts).
**Rows 15–20** as chart, then bind off loosely. Weave in any loose ends using a darning needle (do not just cut them off). Block (see page 155) garment and press carefully on wrong side using a damp cloth.

### Finishing pockets
**Left pocket top** With wrong side facing and size 3 (3¼ mm) needles and C, slip the 46 sts from st holder onto needle and p them. Using 2 strands A, work 8 rows of cable panel as before, then bind off loosely.

**Right pocket lining** With right side facing and size 3 (3¼ mm) needles and C and D, slip the 46 sts from st holder onto needle, then with C cast on 14 sts (60 sts). Work rows 1–32 as chart 2, then bind off loosely. Stitch pocket linings in place carefully, stitching down the 14 sts cast on for right pocket lining along 1st row of panel and stitch down edges of pocket tops.

### Shoulder seams
With right side facing and size 3 (3¼ mm) needles and A, pick up and k 42 sts along right front shoulder. Join on 2nd strand A and p 1 row, then work 8 rows of cable panel as before. Leave sts on a spare needle.
With size 3 (3¼ mm) needles and A, pick up and k 42 sts along right back shoulder and leave sts on needle. Graft (see page 155) right front shoulder to right back shoulder (right sides together). Rep for left shoulder.

### SLEEVES
With size 3 (3¼ mm) needles and A, cast on 125 sts. Work 6 panels – working alternately from charts 1 and 2, beginning chart 1 at st 1, row 1, and chart 2 at st 26, row 1. Beg with chart 1, and work color combinations for chart B as follows:
Panels 2 and 6 in E and shades of F and panel 4 in C and shades of D – work 8 rows of cable panel in 2 strands A between each panel as before and end with 8 rows of cable panel in A. Leave sts on needle. Press on wrong side using a damp cloth.
Make a box pleat by folding panels 3 and 5 in half and bringing the folded edges tog at centre of panel 4. Stitch pleat down neatly at top and bottom edges of sleeve.

## Cuffs

With right side facing and size 2 (2¼ mm) needles and A, pick up and k 160 sts along lower edge of sleeve.
**Dec row 1** *k2 tog; rep from * to end (80 sts).
**Dec row 2** *k2, k2 tog; rep from * to end (60 sts).
**Rows 3–5** k.
Join on B and work from chart 1, beg at st 1, row 9.
**Rows 9–33** work as chart. K 1 row with A.
Then k 6 rows, join on 2nd strand A and cast off loosely purlwise. Graft (see page 155) sts on needle to sts of cast-on edge (right sides tog). Using small back st and matching chevrons, sew edges of cuff together.

## WELT

Make a box pleat at centre back by folding panels 5 and 7 in half and bringing folded edges tog at centre of panel 6. Stitch pleat down at top and bottom edges. With right side facing and size 2 (2¼ mm) needles and A, pick up and k 320 sts (through all layers of pleat) along lower edge of fronts and back. Join on 2nd strand A and k 5 rows. Join on B. Turn chart upside down and, beg with a k row, work from row 40 back to row 1 to reverse direction of chevron. Break off B, k 8 rows with A, then bind off loosely knitwise.

## NECKBAND

With right side facing and size 2 (2¼ mm) needles and A, pick up and k 120 sts around neck. K 5 rows, then join on B and work rows 13–27 as chart 1. Break off B, then in A p 1 row, k 4 rows. Join on 2nd strand A and bind off loosely purlwise.

## BUTTONHOLE BAND

With right side facing and size 2 (2¼ mm) needles and A, pick up and k 200 sts up right front edge. Join on 2nd strand A.
**Rows 1–3** k.
**Row 4** k 4 sts, bind off 6, *k 25 (including st on needle), bind off 6; rep from * to last 4 sts, k 4.
**Row 5** k, casting on 6 sts over the 7 buttonholes.
**Rows 6–8** k. Bind off loosely knitwise.

## BUTTON BAND

With right side facing and size 2 (2¼ mm) needles and A, pick up and k 200 sts down left front edge. Join on 2nd strand A and k 8 rows, then bind off loosely knitwise. Sew on buttons.

## SLEEVE INSERTION

**Remember** when using a circular needle, k every round.
With right side facing and size 3 (3¼ mm) circular needle and A, pick up and k 135 sts around top edge of sleeve. Join on 2nd strand A and work 8 rounds of cable panel, then bind off loosely.
With size 3 (3¼ mm) circular needle and A, pick up and k 135 sts around armhole. Leave sts on needle and graft (see page 155) to bound-off edge of cable panel of sleeve, matching underarm panels and pleat with center of cable panel at shoulder seam. Weave in loose ends.

# PINKS AND RIBBONS JACKET

Part of the pleasure of working with a team of knitters is that each person can suggest ideas which eventually become a design. In this case it was the ultimate romantic combination of ribbons and roses, but however much I drew it on graph paper the shape refused to balance. Then the roses became pinks, I joined the bows with a vertical ribbon, and suddenly the design fell into place. The ruffles are all picked up after the main bulk of the knitting is completed. The coat is both feminine and versatile, and can be worn with scruffy jeans or a silk evening dress. If you don't squeeze the wool too thoroughly when dyeing it in the indigo it will emerge as a multitude of uneven blues, making it more fun to knit and visually more exciting.

## MATERIALS
Pair of size 2 (2¼ mm) needles
Set of 4 double-pointed size 2 (2¼ mm) needles
Circular size 2 (2¼ mm) needle
Pair of size 3 (3¼ mm) needles
Set of 4 double-pointed size 3 (3¼ mm) needles
Circular size 3 (3¼ mm) needle 29 in (73.5 cm) long
  (optional)
6 buttons

## WEIGHT OF YARN AND COLORS
Gray (A)   6 oz (170 g)
Medium indigo blue (B)   6 oz (170 g)
Dark indigo blue (C)   4 oz (115 g)
Redwood pink (D1)   2 oz (57 g)
Crimson (D2)   2 oz (57 g)
Magenta (D3)   2 oz (57 g)
Red (D4)   2 oz (57 g)
Blue-green (E)   4 oz (115 g)

CHART A

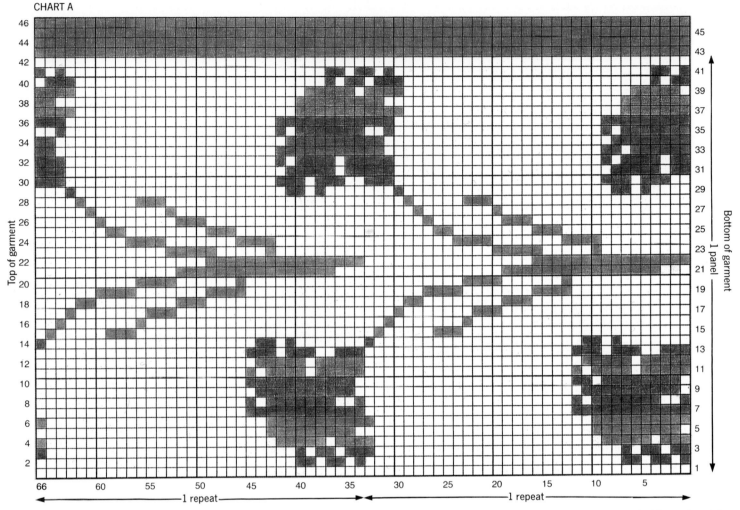

Even-numbered rows are purl, worked from left to right.  Odd-numbered rows are knit, worked from right to left.

## MEASUREMENTS

Length from top of shoulder to bottom edge of cardigan: 21 in (53.5 cm)
Actual width all around at underarm: 46 in (117 cm)
Sleeve length: 22½ in (57 cm)

## GAUGE

Over pattern, using size 3 (3¼ mm) needles (or size to obtain correct gauge), 30 sts and 32 rows to 4 in (10 cm).

## IMPORTANT

● Change shade of red on pinks and ribbons motifs every 2–3 rows to give a random effect.
● Twist wools at back of work every 1–2 sts to avoid making holes, but do not pull tight.
● When working St st using just one color, twist a spare ball of the same color yarn across the back of work to keep the thickness of the garment even.
● This garment is knitted sideways, beginning at the left front edge; the sleeves are also knitted sideways.

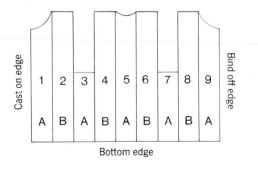

Bottom edge

● There are two background colors so always check that you are using the correct color: panels 1, 3, 5, 7, and 9 are in A and panels 2, 4, 6, and 8 are in B.

## INSTRUCTIONS
### FRONTS AND BACK
#### Panel 1

With size 3 (3¼ mm) needles and A, cast on 104 sts. K 1 row, p 1 row, then work 12 rows as chart A, beg at st 20, row 15.

Cont working from chart, and beg with a right side row, inc alternate rows to shape neck as follows:
**Rows 27 and 29** inc 1 st at end (neck edge) of row.
**Rows 31 and 33** cast on 2 sts at end (neck edge) of row.
**Rows 35 and 37** cast on 3 sts at end (neck edge) of row.
**Rows 39 and 41** cast on 5 sts at end (neck edge) of row (126 sts).
**Row 42** as chart. Work 4 rows rev St st in C as follows:
**Row 1** k.
**Row 2** k.
**Row 3** p.
**Row 4** k.

#### Panel 2

Join on B and work from chart B, beg at st 10, row 1.
**Rows 1–41** as chart.
**Row 42** With wrong side facing bind off 52 sts (neck edge), patt to end (74 sts).
Join on C and work 4 rows rev St st as before.

CHART B

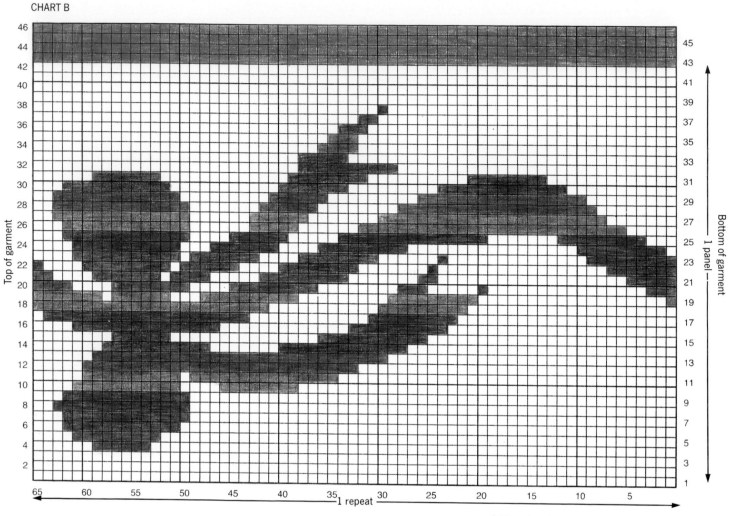

Odd-numbered rows are knit, worked from right to left.
Even-numbered rows are purl, worked from left to right.

### Panel 3 (underarm panel)
Join on A and work from chart A, beg at st 20, row 1.
**Rows 1–42** as chart. Join on C and work 4 rows rev St st as before.

### Panel 4
Join on B and work from chart B, beg at st 10, row 1.
**Row 1** Patt to end (neck edge), then cast on 52 sts (126 sts).
**Rows 2–42** as chart, then join on C and work 4 rows rev St st as before.

### Panel 5
Join on A and work from chart A, beg at st 20, row 1, dec 1 st at end (neck edge) of first and every following 4th row until 122 sts rem. Then work straight until row 29 of chart has been worked.
**Row 30** inc 1 st at the beg (neck edge) of this and every following 4th row until there are 126 sts, then join on C and work 4 rows rev St st as before.

### Panel 6
Join on B and work from chart B, beg at st 10, row 1.
**Rows 1–41** as chart.
**Row 42** cast off 52 sts (neck edge), patt to end (74 sts).
Join on C and work 4 rows rev St st as before.

### Panel 7 (underarm panel)
Join on A and work from chart A, beg at st 20, row 1.
**Rows 1–42** as chart. Join on C and work 4 rows rev St st as before.

### Panel 8
Join on B and work from chart B, beg at st 10, row 1.
**Row 1** Patt to end (neck edge) then cast on 52 sts (126 sts).
**Rows 2–42** as chart. Join on C and work 4 rows rev St st as before.

### Panel 9
Join on A and work from chart A, beg at st 20, row 1.
**Row 1** as chart.
Cont working from chart, dec alternate rows as follows:
**Rows 2 and 4** bind off 5 sts (neck edge), patt to end.
**Rows 6 and 8** bind off 3 sts (neck edge), patt to end.
**Rows 10 and 12** bind off 2 sts (neck edge), patt to end.
**Rows 14 and 16** bind off 1 st (neck edge), patt to end (104 sts).
**Rows 17–28** as chart. Using A, k 1 row and p 1 row. Bind off loosely. Weave in any loose ends using a darning needle (do not just cut them off). Block (see page 155) garment and press carefully on wrong side using a damp cloth.

### Shoulder seams
With right side facing and size 2 (2¼ mm) size 13) needles and C, pick up and k 40 sts along right front shoulder. K 1 row, p 1 row and k 1 row. Leave sts on a spare needle for grafting.

With right side facing and size 2 (2¼ mm) needles and C, pick up and k 40 sts along right back shoulder and leave sts on needle for grafting. Graft (see page 155) right front shoulder to right back shoulder (right sides together). Rep for left shoulder.

## SLEEVES

With size 3 (3¼ mm) needles and A, cast on 133 sts. Work 4 complete panels with 4 rows rev St st in C between each panel, beg with 4 rows rev St st, working from charts in following order:

Panel 1 (underarm panel) chart A, beg at st 22, row 1.
Panel 2 chart B, beg at st 8, row 1.
Panel 3 chart A, beg at st 22, row 1.
Panel 4 chart B, beg at st 8, row 1.

Keep sts on needle. Weave in any loose ends using a darning needle (do not just cut them off). Press carefully on wrong side using a damp cloth. Graft (see page 155) cast on edge of sleeve to sts on needle (right sides together).

## Cuffs

With right side facing, making sure patt is right way up, and set of 4 double-pointed size 2 (2¼ mm) needles and C, pick up and k 122 sts around lower edge of sleeve. Join.

Round 1 *k2 tog; rep from * to end (61 sts).
Round 2 *k4, k2 tog; rep from * to last 7 sts, k4, k3 tog (50 sts). Work 24 rounds in k1 p1 rib, looping short strand brightly colored wool around 1st and last st of round 24 as a marker. Then work 2 rounds in k1 p1 rib.
Frill 1 Change to set of 4 double-pointed size 3 (3¼ mm) needles and work 1 round, inc into every st (100 sts), then join on E.
Next round work 1 row in k1 p1 rib.
Next round p, then bind off loosely knitwise.
Frill 2 With set of 4 double-pointed size 2 (2¼ mm) needles and C, pick up and k 50 sts along round indicated by marker on inside of Cuff. Work 5 rounds in k1 p1 rib, then change to set of 4 double-pointed size 3 (3¼ mm) needles and work 1 round, inc into every st (100 sts). Join on A.
Next round work 1 round in k1 p1 rib.
Next round p, then bind off loosely knitwise.
Frill 3 With set of 4 double-pointed size 2 (2¼ mm) needles and C, pick up and k 50 sts along round indicated by marker on inside of cuff (this is exactly the same place as for Frill 2). Work 9 rounds in k1 p1 rib, then change to set of 4 double-pointed size 3 (3¼ mm) needles and work 1 round, inc into every st (100 sts).
Next round Join on D and work 1 round in k1 p1 rib.
Next round p, then bind off loosely knitwise.

## WELT

With right side facing and size 2 (2¼ mm) needles and C, pick up and k 230 sts along lower edge of fronts and back and work 24 rows in k1 p1 rib. Loop short strand

brightly colored wool round 1st and last sts of row 24 as markers.
Frill 1 Change to size 3 (3¼ mm) needles and work 1 row, inc into every st (460 sts). (Tip: slip sts onto size 3 (3¼ mm) circular needle as this will accommodate all the sts more comfortably and just k from it lengthwise.) Join on E.
Next row work 1 row in k1 p1 rib.
Next row With wrong side facing k 1 row, then cast off loosely purlwise.
Frill 2 With size 2 (2¼ mm) needles and C, pick up and k 230 sts along row indicated by markers on inside of Welt. Work 5 rows in k1 p1 rib then change to size 3 (3¼ mm) needles (or circular needle as before) and work 1 row, inc into every st (460 sts). Join on A.
Next row work 1 row in k1 p1 rib.
Next row k, then bind off loosely purlwise.
Frill 3 With size 2 (2¼ mm) needles and C, pick up and k 230 sts along row indicated by markers on inside of Welt (this is exactly the same place as for Frill 2). Work 9 rows in k1 p1 rib, then change to size 3 (3¼ mm) needles (or circular needle as before) and work 1 row, inc into every st (460 sts). Join on D.
Next row work 1 row in k1 p1 rib.
Next row k, then bind off loosely purlwise.

## NECKBAND

With size 2 (2¼ mm) needles and C, pick up and k 110 sts around neck, beg at right front neck edge (right side facing).
Work 5 rows in k1 p1 rib.
Frill 1 Change to size 3 (3¼ mm) needles and work 1 row, inc into every st to end, then pick up and k 4 sts down side of ribbing (224 sts). Join on A.
Next row work in k1 p1 rib to end and then pick up and k 4 sts down side of ribbing (228 sts), then k 1 row and bind off loosely purlwise.
Frill 2 Turn Frill 1 down onto right side of work and with size 2 (2¼ mm) needles and C, pick up and k 110 sts on inside of neckband in exactly the same place as Frill 1. Work 7 rows in k1 p1 rib, then change to size 3 (3¼ mm) needles and work 1 row, inc into every st to end, and then pick up and k 6 sts down side of ribbing (226 sts). Join on D.
Next row work in k1 p1 rib to end and then pick up and k 6 sts down side of ribbing (232 sts), then k 1 more row and bind off loosely purlwise.
Frill 3 Turn Frills 1 and 2 down onto right side of work and with size 2 (2¼ mm) needles and C, pick up and k 110 sts on inside of neckband in exactly the same place as Frills 1 and 2. Work 11 rows in k1 p1 rib, then change to size 3 (3¼ mm) needles and work 1 row, inc into every st to end, and then pick up and k 10 sts down side of ribbing (230 sts). Join on E.
Next row work in k1 p1 rib to end and then pick up and k 10 sts down side of ribbing (240 sts), then k 1 more row and bind off loosely purlwise.

## BUTTONHOLE BAND

Frill With size 2 (2¼ mm) needles and C, pick up and k 104 sts between top of welt and neck edge (do not include the welt). Work 4 rows in k1 p1 rib, then change to size 3 (3¼ mm) needles and work 1 row, inc into every st, then pick up and k 4 sts down side of ribbing (212 sts). Join on E.
Next row work in k1 p1 rib to end and then pick up and k 4 sts down side of ribbing (216 sts), then k 1 row and bind off loosely purlwise.
Turn Frill down onto right side of work and with size 2 (2¼ mm) needles and C, pick up and k 125 sts in exactly the same place, including Welt and Frills, beg just inside inc row of Frill 1.
Rows 1–3 work in k1 p1 rib, then make buttonholes.
Row 4 rib 2, bind off 6, *rib until there are 17 sts on right-hand needle, bind off 6; rep from * to last 2 sts, rib 2.
Row 5 cont in k1 p1 rib, casting on 6 sts over the 6 buttonholes.
Rows 6–9 work in k1 p1 rib.
Row 10 p (to make foldline).
Rows 11–14 work in k1 p1 rib.
Rows 15 and 16 as rows 4 and 5.
Rows 17–19 work in k1 p1 rib, then bind off loosely in rib. Fold band to inside along foldline and stitch down neatly, neatening around buttonholes with a small buttonhole st.

## BUTTON BAND

Frill Work exactly as given for Buttonhole band Frill. Turn Frill down onto right side of work and with size 2 (2¼ mm) needles and C, pick up and k 126 sts in exactly the same place, including Welt and Frills, then work 9 rows in k1 p1 rib. P next row (to make foldline), work 9 more rows in k1 p1 rib, then bind off loosely in rib. Fold band to inside along foldline and stitch down neatly. Sew on buttons.

## SLEEVE INSERTION

With size 2 (2¼ mm) circular needle and C, pick up and k 132 sts around top edge of sleeve. Loop a short strand of brightly colored wool around 1st st of round as a marker and then p 4 rounds. Leave sts on needle. Place sleeve in armhole with right sides tog, matching underarm panels, and graft (see page 155) tog.
Frill With set of 4 double-pointed size 2 (2¼ mm) needles and C, pick up and k 104 sts around top edge of sleeve, except underarm panel, along round indicated by marker. Work 4 rows in k1 p1 rib, then change to size 3 (3¼ mm) needles and work 1 row, inc into every st, and then pick up and k 4 sts down side of ribbing (212 sts). Join on E.
Next row work in k1 p1 rib to end and then pick up and k 4 sts down side of ribbing (216 sts), then k 1 more row and bind off loosely purlwise.
Rep for 2nd sleeve.

# MAGICIAN SWEATER

Of all my designs, this has been the most fun to create. Who could resist rearranging the heavens and playing with sparkling stars and moons? It uses plied wool, which is thicker than unplied, and is quickly knitted. The sleeves taper at the wrist. The variegated stars and moons leave you free to experiment with the sparkling effect, which can be brightened or subdued according to how you mix the colors. I like using the dark colors on the outside of the motifs, working gradually to a pale center. Women can wear this roomy sweater as easily as men. Some of the dye recipes can be doubled up, which will save time.

**MATERIALS**

Circular size 2 (2¼ mm) needle 29 in (73.5 cm) long
Set of 4 double-pointed size 2 (2¼ mm) needles
2 circular size 6 (4 mm) needles 16 in (40 cm) and 29 in (73.5 cm) long
Pair of size 6 (4 mm) needles
8 stitch holders

Top of garment

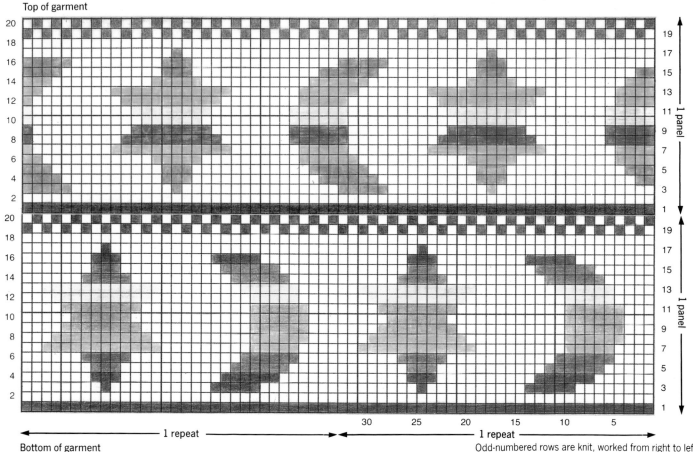

1 repeat

1 repeat

Bottom of garment

Odd-numbered rows are knit, worked from right to left.
Even-numbered rows are purl, worked from left to right.

## WEIGHT OF YARN AND COLORS
Plied yarn
**Navy (A)**  12 oz (345 g)
**Dark gray (B)**  8 oz (230 g)
**Gray (C)**  8 oz (230 g)
**Dark indigo blue (D)**  6 oz (170 g)
**Ochre (E1)**  3 oz (85 g)
**Red (E2)**  2 oz (57 g)
**Walnut (E3)**  3 oz (85 g)
**Yellow (E4)**  3 oz (85 g)
**Natural (E5)**  3 oz (85 g)

## MEASUREMENTS
Length from top of shoulder to bottom edge of sweater:
30 in (76 cm)
Actual width all around at underarm: 48 in (122 cm)
Sleeve length: 26 in (65 cm)

## GAUGE
Over pattern, using size 6 (4 mm) needles (or size to
obtain gauge), 23 stitches and 24 rows to 4 in (10 cm).

## IMPORTANT
● Change colors of wool for star and moon motifs
every 2–3 rows to give a random effect.
● Twist wools at back of work every 1–2 stitches to

avoid making holes, but do not pull tight.
● When working St st using just one color, twist a
spare ball of the same color yarn across the back of
work to keep the thickness of the garment even.
● The sweater is knitted on a circular needle as far as
the underarm, so every round of the chart up to that
point is knit.
● When using circular needles, take great care on the
first round to make sure that the stitches are not twisted
around the needle.
● When knitting in the round, loop a short strand of
brightly colored wool around the first stitch each time
you begin a round so that you can find the beginning.
● The sleeves are knitted on a circular needle and
worked from shoulder to cuff, so remember to reverse
the order of the pattern, that is, work from row 20–1.
● There are 4 background colors so always check that
you are using the correct color as follows:

| BODY | SLEEVE (top to bottom) |
|---|---|
| Panel 1: A | Panel 1: A |
| Panel 2: B | Panel 2: B |
| Panel 3: C | Panel 3: C |
| Panel 4: D | Panel 4: D |
| Panel 5: C | Panel 5: C |
| Panel 6: B | Panel 6: B |
| Panel 7: A | Panel 7: A |
| Panel 8: B | |

## INSTRUCTIONS
### FRONT AND BACK
With size 2 (2¼ mm) circular needle and A, cast on 240
sts. Work 24 rounds in k1 p1 rib.
**Inc round** *k4, inc into next st; rep from * to end (288
sts).
Change to size 6 (4 mm) 29 in (73.5 cm) long circular
needle and work panels 1 and 2 alternately for 100
rounds. (Work panels 1 and 2 alternately throughout
pattern.)

### Divide for front and back
Slip first 14 sts onto a st holder (Holder 1) for underarm,
then patt 116 sts.
Leave rem sts on circular needle and, with pair of size 6
(4 mm) needles, work straight on these 116 sts for
back, until 3 complete panels and 1 row have been
worked.
**Row 2** (wrong side facing) patt 39 sts, turn.
**Row 3** k2 tog, patt to end.
**Row 4** patt 38 sts, turn.
**Row 5** k2 tog, patt to end (37 sts), then slip these 37
sts onto a st holder for left back shoulder.
With wrong side facing, slip next 38 sts onto a st holder
for back neck, then cont on rem 39 sts as follows:
**Row 2** (wrong side facing) patt to end.
**Row 3** patt to last 2 sts, k2 tog, turn.

**Row 4** as chart.
**Row 5** patt to last 2 sts, k2 tog, turn (37 sts), then slip sts onto a st holder for right back shoulder.
With right side facing, return to rem sts and slip next 28 sts onto a st holder (Holder 2) for underarm. Patt 116 sts and slip rem 14 sts onto Holder 1.
With pair of size 6 (4 mm) needles, work 2 complete panels and 4 rows.
**Row 5** patt 43 sts, turn.
**Row 6** bind off 2 sts, patt to end.
**Row 7** as chart.
**Row 8** bind off 2 sts, patt to end.
**Row 9** as chart.
**Row 10** bind off 1 st, patt to end.
**Row 11** as chart.
**Row 12** bind off 1 st, patt to end (37 sts).
Work straight until rest of this panel and 6 rows of next have been worked, then slip sts onto a st holder for left front shoulder. Slip next 30 sts onto a st holder for front neck and then work rem 43 sts (right side facing) as follows:
**Row 5** bind off 2 sts, patt to end.
**Row 6** as chart.
**Row 7** bind off 2 sts, patt to end.

**Row 8** as chart.
**Row 9** bind off 1 st, patt to end.
**Row 10** as chart.
**Row 11** bind off 1 st, patt to end (37 sts) and then work straight until work matches left side of neck. Leave sts on a spare needle for right front shoulder.

### Shoulder seams
Block (see page 155) garment and press carefully on wrong side using a damp cloth. Graft (see page 155) 37 sts for right front shoulder to right back shoulder and left front shoulder to left back shoulder (right sides together). Weave in any loose ends using darning needle (do not just cut them off).

### SLEEVES
**Remember** to k all rounds and panels in rev order – from row 20–1.
With right side facing and size 6 (4 mm) 16 in (40 cm) circular needle and A, slip last 14 sts from Holder 1 onto left needle and k them. Then pick up and k 66 sts up to shoulder seam, 66 sts down to st holder and then k the 14 sts left on Holder (160 sts). Then work from chart, beg at st 32, row 19, until 2 complete panels and rows

20–3 of next panel have been worked.
**Row 2** *k3, k2 tog; rep from * to end (128 sts), then work straight until 4 complete panels and rows 20–3 (counting from beg) have been worked.
**Row 2** *k2, k2 tog; rep from * to end (96 sts), then work straight until 6 complete panels and rows 20–3 (counting from beg) have been worked. Change to set of 4 double-pointed size 2 (2¼ mm) needles.
**Row 2** *k1, k2 tog; rep from * to end (64 sts), then work 24 rounds in A in k1 p1 rib, then bind off loosely in rib. Weave in any loose ends using a darning needle. Press sleeves carefully on wrong side using a damp cloth.

### NECKBAND
With right side facing and set of 4 double-pointed size 2 (2¼ mm) needles and A, k the 38 sts for back of neck, pick up and k 27 sts down left side of neck, k the 30 sts for front of neck and pick up and k 27 sts up right side of neck (right side facing; 122 sts). Work 9 rounds in k1 p1 rib. P next round (to make foldline) and work 9 more rounds in k1 p1 rib, then bind off loosely in rib. Fold band to inside along foldline and stitch down neatly.

# STARS AND MOONS HAT

## MATERIALS
Pair of size 8 (5 mm) needles
Approximately 4 ft by 2¾ in (130 by 7 cm) strip of 4 oz (115 g) polyester padding
Piece of medium-weight cardboard (large enough to accommodate 6 circles each 3 in [8 cm] in diameter)

## WEIGHT OF YARN AND COLORS
**PLIED YARN** (or 2 strands of ordinary yarn knitted together)
**Navy (A)** 3 oz (85 g)
**Dark indigo blue (B)** 3 oz (85 g)
**Yellow (C)** 3 oz (85 g)
**Gray (D)** ½ oz (14 g)
**Walnut (E)** ¼ oz (14 g)

## GAUGE
Over pattern, using size 8 (5 mm) needles (or size to obtain gauge), 18 stitches and 24 rows to 4 in (10 cm).

## INSTRUCTIONS

### BRIM
With size 8 (5 mm) needles and A, cast on 48 sts and work from chart, beg at st 1, row 1.
**Rows 1 and 2** as chart.
**Row 3** dec 1 st at beg of row and inc 1 st at end of row.
**Row 4** as chart.
**Rows 5–86** as chart, dec and inc each alternate row as row 3, then bind off loosely in A. Weave in any loose ends using a darning needle (do not just cut them off) and press carefully on wrong side using a damp cloth. Bring cast on edge and bound-off edge tog (right sides tog) and sew neat seam using small backstitches.

### CROWN
With size 8 (5 mm) needles and B, cast on 104 sts and work 40 rows in St st, then shape each alternate row as follows (right side facing):

**Row 1** k5, *k3 tog, k10*; rep from * to last 8 sts, k3 tog, k5 (88 sts).
**Row 2** (and each alternate row) p.
**Row 3** k4, *k3 tog, k8; rep from * to last 7 sts, k3 tog, k4 (72 sts).
**Row 5** k3, *k3 tog, k6*; rep from * to last 6 sts, k3 tog, k3 (56 sts).
**Row 7** k2, *k3 tog, k4*; rep from * to last 5 sts, k3 tog, k2 (40 sts).
**Row 9** k1, *k3 tog, k2*; rep from * to last 4 sts. K3 tog, k1 (24 sts).
**Row 11** *k3 tog*; rep from * to * to end (8 sts). Keep sts on needle. Cut off wool, leaving a length of about 4 in (10 cm), then, using a darning needle, thread this through sts on needle, pull tightly and fasten off securely. Bring side edges of crown tog (right sides tog) and sew a neat seam using small backstitches.

### FINISHING
Place left-hand edge of brim (wrong side facing) along inside cast-on edge of crown (wrong side facing), matching brim seam with crown seam, and sew neat seam using small backstitches. Fold strip of padding in half lengthwise and lay it on wrong side of brim below seam. Bring right-hand edge of brim up over padding and slip stitch it to cast-on edge of crown. Then, with tiny, loose slip stitches, stitch brim to crown again about 2 cm (¾ in) up from cast-on edge of crown.

Cast off edge

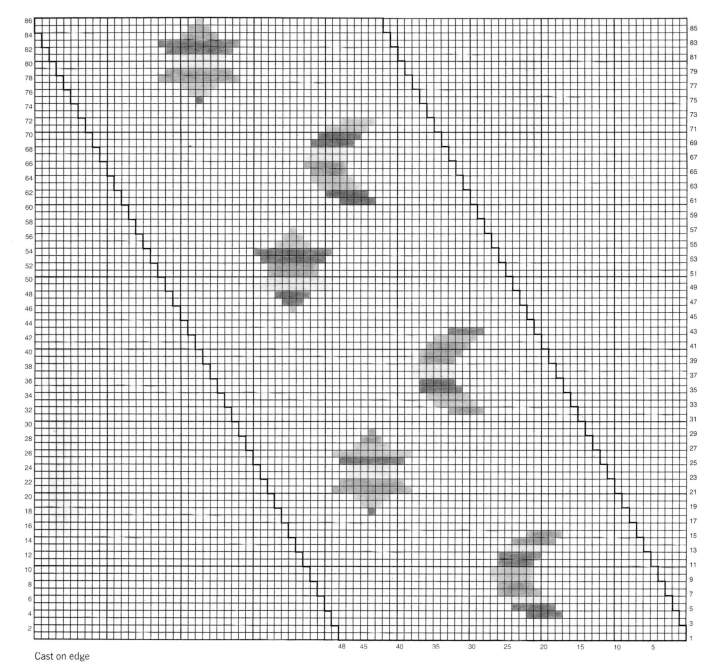

Cast on edge

## Pompons

With A, make 3 braids (9, 12, and 15½ in; 23, 31, and 39 cm long), using 3 strands of yarn for each braid. Put aside.

Cut out 6 circles from the cardboard, approximately 3 in (8 cm) in diameter. In the center of each circle mark another, approximately ¾ in (2 cm) in diameter, and cut them out. Place 2 of the cardboard rings tog and, using one of the colors you used for the moon and star motifs, thread a darning needle and wind it evenly around the cardboard ring, from inner to outer edge, until the inner circle is tightly filled (make any knots on outer edge of ring). Then insert the tip of some sharp scissors between the 2 cardboard rings and cut the wool all around the outer edge. Pull the 2 cardboard rings slightly apart and tie a length of the same color wool tightly around all the strands of wool in the middle. Attach 1 end of 1 of the braids securely to this, then tear off the 2 cardboard rings. Snip off any uneven ends around pompon so you have a good smooth shape. Make 2 more pompons in the same way and then attach braids securely to top of hat by passing them through hole and stitching them to side seam.

# POPPIES CARDIGAN

Only a small amount of dyeing is required for this cardigan, as the background is natural. The knitting is done sideways, and it is important to weave the wool to the end of each row or the gauge goes completely crazy. The poppies are bold and stand out well against the background. It's a cardigan I wear a lot on cool summer evenings.

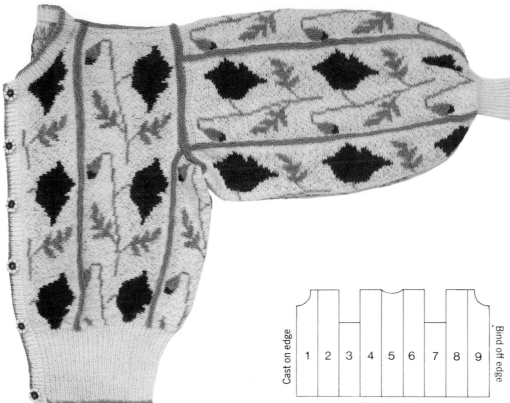

## MATERIALS

Pair of size 2 (2¼ mm) needles
Set of 4 double-pointed size 2 (2¼ mm) needles
Pair of size 3 (3¼ mm) needles
6 buttons

## WEIGHT OF YARN AND COLORS

Natural (A)    12 oz (340 g)
Blue-green (B)    6 oz (170 g)
Crimson (C)    4 oz (115 g)
Burgundy (D)    1½ oz (42 g)

## MEASUREMENTS

Length from top of shoulder to bottom edge of cardigan: 22½ in (57 cm)
Actual width all around at underarm: 50 in (127 cm)
Sleeve length: 22 in (56 cm)

## GAUGE

Over pattern, using size 3 (3¼ mm) needles (or size to obtain gauge), 28 sts and 30 rows to 4 in (10 cm).

## IMPORTANT

• Twist wools at back of work every 1–2 sts to avoid making holes, but do not pull tight.
• When working St st using just one color, twist a spare ball of the same color yarn across the back of work to keep the thickness of the garment even.
• This garment is knitted sideways, beginning at left front edge, and the sleeves are also knitted sideways.

## INSTRUCTIONS
### FRONTS AND BACK
**Panel 1**

With size 3 (3¼ mm) needles and A, cast on 104 sts.

Work 2 rows in St st, then work from chart, beg at st 21, row 19.
**Rows 19–26** as chart.
Cont working from chart, inc alternate rows as follows:
**Rows 27 and 29** With right side facing inc 1 st at end (neck edge) of row.
**Rows 31 and 33** cast on 2 sts at end (neck edge) of row.
**Rows 35 and 37** cast on 3 sts at end (neck edge) of row.
**Rows 39 and 41** cast on 5 sts at end (neck edge) of row (126 sts).
**Row 42** as chart, then work 4 rows rev St st in B as follows:
**Row 1** k.
**Row 2** k.
**Row 3** p.
**Row 4** k.

**Panel 2**
Work from chart, beg at st 21, row 1.
**Rows 1–41** as chart, omitting stem beg 4th poppy.
**Row 42** With wrong side facing bind off 52 sts (neck edge), patt to end (74 sts), then work 4 rows rev St st in B as before.

**Panel 3** (underarm panel)
Work from chart, beg at st 21, row 1.
**Rows 1–42** as chart, omitting stem beg 3rd poppy, then work 4 rows rev St st in B as before.

**Panel 4**
Work from chart, beg at st 21, row 1.
**Row 1** Patt to end of row (neck edge), cast on 52 sts (126 sts).
**Rows 2–42** as chart, omitting stem beg 4th poppy, then work 4 rows rev St st in B as before.

**Panel 5**
Work from chart, beg at st 21, row 1.
**Rows 1–2** as chart.
**Rows 3–11** dec 1 st at end (neck edge) of 1st and every following 4th row (123 sts).
**Rows 12–31** as chart.
**Rows 32–40** inc 1 st at beg (neck edge) of 32nd and every following 4th row (126 sts), omitting stem beg 4th poppy.
**Rows 41–42** as chart.
Work 4 rows rev St st in B as before.

**Panel 6**
Work from chart, beg at st 21, row 1.
**Rows 1–41** as chart, omitting stem beg 4th poppy.
**Row 42** With wrong side facing bind off 52 sts (neck

Cast on edge

| 1 | 2 | 3 | 4 | 5 | 6 | 7 | 8 | 9 |

Bind off edge

Bottom edge

edge), patt to end (74 sts), then work 4 rows rev St st in B as before.

### Panel 7 (underarm panel)
Work from chart, beg at st 21, row 1.
**Rows 1–42** as chart, omitting stem beg 3rd poppy, then work 4 rows rev St st in B as before.

### Panel 8
Work from chart, beg at st 21, row 1.
**Row 1** Patt to end of row (neck edge), cast on 52 sts (126 sts)
**Rows 2–42** as chart, omitting stem beg 4th poppy, then work 4 rows rev St st in B as before.

### Panel 9
Work from chart, beg at st 21, row 1.
**Rows 1–3** as chart.
Cont working from chart, dec alternate rows as follows:
**Rows 4 and 6** bind off 5 sts (neck edge), patt to end.
**Rows 8 and 10** bind off 3 sts (neck edge), patt to end.
**Rows 12 and 14** bind off 2 sts (neck edge), patt to end.
**Rows 16 and 18** bind off 1 st (neck edge), patt to end (104 sts).
**Rows 19–24** as chart. Work 2 rows St st with A, then bind off loosely.
Weave in any loose ends using a darning needle (do not just cut them off). Block (see page 155) garment and press carefully on wrong side using a damp cloth.

### Shoulder seams
With right side facing and size 2 (2¼ mm) needles and B, pick up and k 40 sts along right front shoulder. K 1 row, p 1 row, and k 1 row. Leave sts on a spare needle. With right side facing and size 2 (2¼ mm) needles and B, pick up and k 40 sts along right back shoulder. Leave sts on needle, then graft (see page 155) right front shoulder to right back shoulder (right sides tog). Rep for left shoulder.

### SLEEVES
With size 3 (3¼ mm) needles and A, cast on 133 sts. Work 4 complete panels from chart, beg at st 23, row 1 and omitting stem beg 4th poppy, with 4 rows rev St st in B between each panel and end with 4 rows rev St st. Leave sts on needle, then weave in any loose ends using a darning needle (do not just cut them off). Press carefully on wrong side using a damp cloth. Graft (see page 155) sts on needle to cast on edge (right sides tog).

### Cuffs
With right side facing and set of 4 double-pointed size 2 (2¼ mm) needles and A, pick up and k 122 sts along lower sleeve edge, making sure patt is correct.
**Round 1** *k2 tog; rep from * around (61 sts).
**Round 2** k to last 2 sts, k2 tog (60 sts), then work 43 more rounds in k1 p1 rib. Join on B, work 2 rounds in k1 p1 rib. Join on 2nd strand B, bind off loosely in rib.

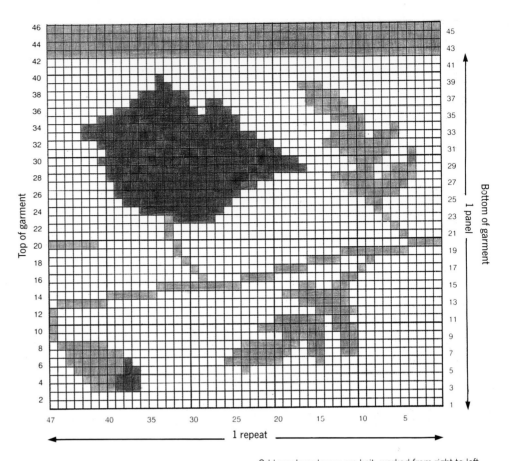

Odd-numbered rows are knit, worked from right to left.
Even-numbered rows are purl, worked from left to right.

### WELT
With right side facing and size 2 (2¼ mm) needles and A, pick up and k 260 sts along lower edge of fronts and back. Work 43 rows in k1 p1 rib, join on B and work 2 rows in k1 p1 rib, then join on 2nd strand B and bind off loosely in rib.

### NECKBAND
With right side facing and size 2 (2¼ mm) needles and A, pick up and k 110 sts around neck. Work 7 rows in k1 p1 rib, then join on B and work 2 rows in k1 p1 rib. P 1 row (to make foldline) then work 2 rows in k1 p1 rib. Join on A and work 7 more rows in k1 p1 rib, then bind off loosely in rib. Fold band to inside along foldline and stitch down neatly.

### BUTTONHOLE BAND
With right side facing and size 2 (2¼ mm) needles and A, pick up and k 147 sts up right front edge.
**Rows 1–4** work in k1 p1 rib, then make buttonholes:
**Row 5** rib 3, bind off 6, *rib 21 (including st on needle), bind off 6; rep from * to last 3 sts, rib 3.
**Row 6** cont in k1 p1 rib, casting on 6 sts over the 6 buttonholes.
**Row 7** work in k1 p1 rib.
**Rows 8–9** join on B and work 2 rows in k1 p1 rib.
**Row 10** p (to make foldline).

**Rows 11–12** work in k1 p1 rib. Break off B.
**Row 13** join on A and work in k1 p1 rib.
**Rows 14–15** as rows 5 and 6.
**Rows 16–19** work in k1 p1 rib, then bind off loosely in rib. Fold band to inside along foldline and stitch down neatly, using small buttonhole stitch around buttonholes.

### BUTTON BAND
With right side facing and size 2 (2¼ mm) needles and A, pick up and k 147 sts down left front edge. Work 7 rows in k1 p1 rib in A, join on B and work 2 more rows in k1 p1 rib. P 1 row (to make foldline) then work 2 more rows in k1 p1 rib. Break off B. Join on A and work 7 more rows in k1 p1 rib, then bind off loosely in rib. Fold band to inside along foldline and stitch down neatly. Sew on buttons.

### SLEEVE INSERTION
With set of 4 double-pointed size 2 (2¼ mm) needles and B, pick up and k 132 sts around top edge of sleeve (right side facing). Work 3 rounds in p, then bind off loosely knitwise. Rep for 2nd sleeve. Place sleeves in armholes with right sides tog, matching underarm panels. Sew seams using small back sts. Weave in loose ends using a darning needle (do not just cut them off).

# ADULT TULIP JACKET

I have a soft spot for the Tulip jacket. It was my first success at creating a design to be used exclusively with natural dyes, one that would show off the range of the colors, and their brightness. The rounded patterning and generous shapes give the tulips a life of their own. It's an enjoyable jacket for a new knitter to tackle: the knitting has a rhythm, and there's freedom to play with the shades of red and pink within the tulips. The blues, grays, and greens are all soft vibrant colors, and the theatrical sleeves add to its impact.

## MATERIALS
Pair of size 2 (2¼ mm) needles
Set of 4 double-pointed size 2 (2¼ mm) needles
2 pairs of size 3 (3¼ mm) needles
Circular size 3 (3¼ mm) needle 16 in (40 cm) long
9 stitch holders
9 buttons

## WEIGHT OF YARN AND COLORS
Green (A)   4 oz (115 g)
Scarlet (B1)   2 oz (57 g)
Crimson (B2)   2 oz (57 g)
Red (B3)   2 oz (57 g)
Dark undigo blue (C)   10 oz (280 g)
Dark gray (D)   8 oz (230 g)
Medium indigo blue (E)   6 oz (170 g)
Gray (F)   4 oz (115 g)

## MEASUREMENTS
Length from top of shoulder to bottom edge of jacket:
30 in (76 cm)
Actual width all around at underarm: 51 in (129.5 cm)
Sleeve length: 22 in (56 cm)

## GAUGE

Over pattern, using size 3 (3¼ mm) needles (or size to obtain gauge), 28 stitches and 32 rows to 4 in (10 cm).

## IMPORTANT

● Change shade of red for tulip motif every 2–3 rows to give a random effect.

● Twist wools at back of work every 1–2 sts to avoid making holes, but do not pull tight.

● When working St st using just one color, twist a spare ball of the same color yarn across the back of work to keep the thickness of the garment even.

● To make ridge on right side of work between each panel, rows 1 and 2 of the chart are knit.

● When using the circular needle for the sleeves, remember that all rounds of chart are knit (except round 1, which is purl) and must be worked in reverse order as you are knitting from shoulder to cuff, that is, you work from row 24 to 1.

● When using the circular needle, loop a short strand of brightly colored wool around the first stitch each time you begin a round so that you can find the beginning easily.

## INSTRUCTIONS

### FRONTS AND BACK

With size 2 (2¼ mm) needles and 2 strands A, cast on 310 sts. Cont with single strand and work 2 rows in k1 p1 rib. Join on B1 and work 2 more rows in k1 p1 rib. Join on C and work 41 more rows in k1 p1 rib.

Inc row rib 20, *inc into next st, rib 4; rep from * to last 20 sts, rib 20 (364 sts). Then join on A, change to size 3 (3¼ mm) needles and work from chart, beg at st 1, row 1, keeping 1st 2 and last 2 sts plain as these are the front edges.

Work 2 complete panels, ending 2nd panel with row 24 and working panel 1 in background color D and panel 2 in background color E.

## Pocket linings

Lay work aside. With size 3 (3¼ mm) needles and background color D, cast on 42 sts. For pocket lining 1, beg at st 28, row 1 of chart, for pocket lining 2, beg at st 22, row 1 and work 2 panels as chart. Leave each pocket lining on one of 2nd pair of size 3 (3¼ mm) needles. Return to main body of work.

Patt 29 sts, slip next 42 sts onto a st holder, then join in pocket lining 1, k from its needle, and patt to last 71 sts. Slip next 42 sts onto a st holder, then join in pocket lining 2, k from its needle, and work to end. Work straight, working panel 3 in background color F, panel 4 in background color C and then rep background colors in same order, until 6 panels, ending panel 6 with row 24, have been worked.

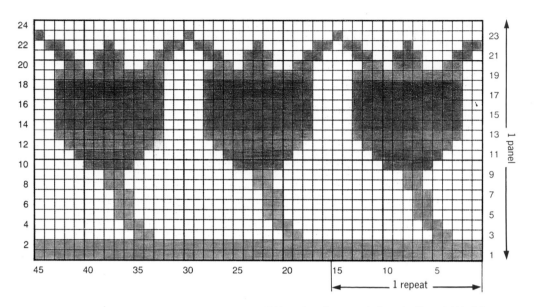

Odd-numbered rows are knit, worked from right to left.
Even-numbered rows are purl, worked from left to right.

## Divide for fronts and back

With right side facing, patt 70 sts, turn. Cont in patt on these 70 sts until 8 panels and 6 rows of panel 9 (counting from beg) have been worked.

Row 7 With right side facing, bind off 16 sts, patt to end (54 sts).

Row 8 patt to last 3 sts, p2 tog, p1.

Row 9 k1, k2 tog, patt to end.

Rep last 2 rows until 44 sts rem.

Work straight until 9th panel has been worked, then k 2 rows with A. Slip these 44 sts onto a st holder, for right front shoulder grafting.

With right side facing return to rem sts. Slip next 42 sts onto a st holder for right underarm and then patt next 140 sts for back and turn. Work straight on these 140 sts until 8 panels and 16 rows (from beg) have been worked.

Row 17 patt 47 sts, k2 tog, k1, turn.

Row 18 p1, p2 tog, patt to end.

Row 19 patt to last 3 sts, k2 tog, k1 (47 sts).

Rep last 2 rows until 44 sts rem, then work straight until 9th panel has been worked. K 1 row with A and slip sts onto a st holder for right back shoulder grafting.

Slip next 40 sts for back neck onto a st holder and work rem 50 sts as follows:

Row 17 k1, k2 tog, patt to end.

Row 18 patt to last 3 sts, p2 tog, p1.

Row 19 k1, k2 tog, patt to end.

Rep last 2 rows until 44 sts rem, then work straight until 9th panel has been worked. K 1 row with A, and slip sts onto a st holder for left back shoulder grafting.

With right side facing, slip next 42 sts onto a st holder for left underarm and then patt rem 70 sts. Work

straight until 8 panels and 5 rows have been worked from beg.

Row 6 bind off 16 sts, patt to end (54 sts).

Row 7 patt to last 3 sts, k2 tog, k1.

Row 8 p1, p2 tog, patt to end.

Rep last 2 rows until 44 sts rem, then work straight until 9th panel has been worked. K2 rows with A, then slip sts onto a st holder for left front shoulder grafting.

## Pocket tops

With right side facing and size 2 (2¼ mm) needles and A, slip the 42 sts for pocket from st holder onto needles and work as follows:

Rows 1 and 2 k.

Rows 3–5 join on C and work in k1 p1 rib.

Rows 6 and 7 join on B1 and work in k1 p1 rib.

Rows 8 and 9 join on A and work in k1 p1 rib, then join on 2nd strand A and bind off loosely in rib.

Stitch down neatly and sew pocket lining into place using a small slip st. Rep for 2nd pocket.

## Shoulder seams

Block (see page 155) garment and press carefully on wrong side using a damp cloth, but do not press ribbing. Graft (see page 155) right front shoulder to right back shoulder (right sides to). Rep for left shoulder. Weave in any loose ends using a darning needle (do not just cut them off).

## SLEEVES

Remember to k all rounds (except round 1 which is p) and work chart in rev order – from row 24–1.

With right side facing and size 3 (3¼ mm) circular

holder onto needle and k them. Then pick up and k 138 sts around armhole and k rem 21 sts on holder (180 sts). P1 round with A. Work 6 complete panels with background colors in the order E, D, C, F, E, and D, ending with round 3. Change to set of 4 double-pointed size 2 (2¼ mm) needles and join on A.

**Dec round 1** *k3, k2 tog; rep from * around (144 sts).
**Dec round 2** *p2, p2 tog; rep from * around (108 sts). Change to C.
**Dec round 3** *k1, k2 tog; rep from * around (72 sts).
**Dec round 4** *k4, k2 tog*; rep from * around (60 sts).
Work 41 rounds in k1 p1 rib in C. Join on B1 and work 2 more rounds in k1 p1 rib, then join on A and work 2 more rounds in rib. Join on 2nd strand A and bind off loosely in rib. Weave in any loose ends using a darning needle (do not just cut them off). Press carefully on wrong side using a damp cloth, but do not press ribbing.

### NECKBAND
With right side facing and size 2 (2¼ mm) needles and C, pick up and k 35 sts between right front neck edge and st holder at back of neck. Slip the 40 sts from holder onto needle and k them, then pick up and k 35 sts down to left front neck edge (110 sts). Work 5 rows in k1 p1 rib, then join on B1 and work 2 rows in rib, then join on A and work 2 rows in rib. P next row (to make foldline), then work 2 rows in rib, then join on B1 and work 2 rows in rib, then join on C and work 5 rows in rib, then bind off loosely in rib. Fold band to inside along foldline and stitch down neatly.

### BUTTONHOLE BAND
With right side facing and size 2 (2¼ mm) needles and C, pick up and k 250 sts up right front.
**Rows 1–3** work in k1 p1 rib, then make buttonholes:
**Row 4** rib 2, bind off 6 sts, *rib 24 (including st left on needle), bind off 6; rep from * to last 2 sts, rib 2.
**Row 5** cont in k1 p1 rib, casting on 6 sts over the 9 buttonholes.
**Rows 6 and 7** join on B1 and work in k1 p1 rib.
**Rows 8 and 9** join on A and work in k1 p1 rib.
**Row 10** p (to make foldline).
**Rows 11 and 12** cont in A k1 p1 rib.
**Rows 13 and 14** join on B1 and work in k1 p1 rib.
**Rows 15 and 16** join on C and work as rows 4 and 5.
**Rows 17–19** work in k1 p1 rib, then bind off loosely in rib. Fold band to inside along foldline and stitch down neatly, using small buttonhole st around buttonholes.

### BUTTON BAND
With right side facing and size 2 (2¼ mm) needles and C, pick up and k 250 sts down left front. Work 5 rows in k1 p1 rib, then join on B1 and work 2 rows in rib, then join on A and work 2 rows in rib. P next row (to make foldline), then work 2 rows in rib, then join on B1 and work 2 rows in rib, then join on C and work 5 rows in rib, then bind off loosely in rib. Fold band to inside along foldline and stitch down neatly. Sew on buttons.

# CHILD'S TULIP CARDIGAN

Of all the flowers used in decoration, the simple shape of the tulip is the most dominant. Tulips embellish European and North American folk art, and stylized versions can be found on furniture, textiles, and ceramics. Its stately silhouette is so obviously floral, and its leaves and stem are easily worked into the pattern. This design evolved out of my first attempt at playing with zeros and crosses on graph paper, and its rounded shape counters the effect of the horizontal lines of the pattern.

### MATERIALS
Pair of size 2 (2¼ mm) needles
Set of 4 double-pointed size 2 (2¼ mm) needles
Pair of size 3 (3¼ mm) needles
Circular size 3 (3¼ mm) needle 16 in (40 cm) long
6 stitch holders
6 buttons

### WEIGHT OF YARN AND COLORS
Blue-green (A)    4 oz (115 g)
Scarlet (B1)    1 oz (28 g)
Crimson (B2)    1 oz (28 g)
Red (B3)    1 oz (28 g)
Magenta (B4)    1 oz (28 g)
Dark indigo blue (C)    4 oz (115 g)
Gray (D)    4 oz (115 g)
Pale indigo blue (E)    2 oz (57 g)

### MEASUREMENTS
Length from top of shoulder to bottom edge of jacket: 15 in (38 cm)
Actual width all around at underarm: 34 in (86 cm)
Sleeve length: 14 in (35.5 cm)

### GAUGE
Over pattern, using size 3 (3¼ mm) needles (or size to obtain gauge), 32 stitches and 32 rows to 4 in (10 cm).

### IMPORTANT
● Change shade of red for tulip motif every 2–3 rows to give a random effect.
● Twist wools at back of work every 1–2 stitches to avoid making holes, but do not pull tight.
● When working ST st using just one colour, twist a spare ball of the same colour yarn across the back of work to keep the thickness of the garment even.
● To make ridge on right side of work between each panel, rows 1 and 2 of the chart are knit.
● When using the circular needle for the sleeves, remember that all rounds of chart are knit (except round 1, which is purl) and must be worked in reverse order as you are knitting from shoulder to cuff, that is, you work from row 24 to 1.
● When using the circular needle, loop a short strand

of brightly colored wool around the first stitch each time you begin a round so that you can find the beginning easily.

### INSTRUCTIONS
#### FRONTS AND BACK
With size 2 (2¼ mm) needles and A, cast on 240 sts and work 2 rows in k1 p1 rib. Join on B1 and work 2 more rows in k1 p1 rib.
Join on C and work 29 more rows in k1 p1 rib.
**Inc row** *rib 7, inc into next st; rep from * to end (270 sts).
Then join on A, change to size 3 (3¼ mm) needles and work from chart, beg at st 1, row 1. Work 2 complete panels, ending 2nd panel with row 24, working panel 1 in background color D, panel 2 in background color E, and tulips in B shades in random numbers of rows.

#### Divide for fronts and back
With right side facing patt 55 sts, turn. Cont in patt on these 55 sts until 3 panels and 10 rows have been worked (from beg), using background color C for panel 3 and background color D for panel 4.
**Row 11** With right side facing, bind off 8 sts, patt to end (47 sts).
**Rows 12–19** dec 1 st at neck edge on every row (39 sts).
**Rows 20–24** as chart. K2 rows with A, then slip sts onto a st holder, for right front shoulder grafting.
With right side facing return to rem 215 sts, slip next 24 sts onto a st holder for right underarm, then patt next 112 sts for back and turn. Work straight on these 112 sts until 3 panels and 16 rows have been worked, working 3rd panel in C and 4th in D.
**Row 17** With right side facing patt 46 sts, turn.
**Rows 18–24** dec 1 st at neck edge on every row (39 sts). K 1 row with A then slip sts onto a st holder for right back shoulder grafting.
Slip next 20 sts onto a st holder for back neck and work rem 46 sts as follows:
**Row 17** patt to end.
**Rows 18–24** dec 1 st at neck edge on every row (39 sts). K 1 row with A then slip sts onto a st holder for left back shoulder grafting.
With right side facing slip next 24 sts onto a st holder for

left underarm, then patt rem 55 sts. Cont in patt in C and complete panel, then work rows 1–11 of next panel in D.

**Row 12** With wrong side facing bind off 8 sts, patt to end (47 sts)

**Rows 13–20** dec 1 st at neck edge every row (39 sts).

**Rows 21–24** as chart. K 2 rows with A. Leave sts on needle for left front shoulder grafting.

### Shoulder seams

Block (see page 155) garment and press carefully on wrong side using a damp cloth. Graft (see page 155) right front shoulder to right back shoulder (right sides together). Rep for left shoulder. Weave in any loose ends using a darning needle (do not just cut them off).

### SLEEVES

**Remember** to k all rounds (except round 1, which is p) and work chart in rev order – from row 24–1.

Slip last 12 sts from st holder for underarm onto size 3 (3¼ mm) circular needle, join on D and k them. Then pick up and k 48 sts up side of armhole between st holder and top of shoulder, pick up and k 48 sts down side of armhole to st holder and k rem 12 sts on holder (120 sts). Work 4 complete panels with background colors in the order D, C, E, and D, ending with round 5. Change to set of 4 double-pointed size 2 (2¼ mm) needles.

**Round 4** *k1, k2 tog; rep from * to end (80 sts).

**Round 3** *k2, k2 tog; rep from * to end (60 sts).

**Round 2** k with A.

**Round 1** p with A.

Work 30 rounds in k1 p1 rib in C. Join on B1 and work 2 more rounds in k1 p1 rib, then join on A and work 2 more rounds in k1 p1 rib. Join on 2nd strand A and bind off loosely in rib. Weave in any loose ends using a darning needle (do not just cut them off). Press carefully on wrong side using a damp cloth, but do not press ribbing.

### NECKBAND

With right side facing and size 2 (2¼ mm) needles and C, pick up and k 37 sts between front neck edge and st holder at back of neck. Slip the 20 sts from st holder onto needle and k them, then pick up and k 37 sts down to left front neck edge (94 sts). Work 5 rows in k1 p1 rib, then join on B1 and work 2 rows in rib, then join on A and work 2 rows in rib. P next row (to make foldline), then work 2 rows in rib, then join on B1 and work 2 rows in rib, then join on C and work 5 rows in rib, then bind off loosely in rib. Fold band to inside along foldline and stitch down neatly.

### BUTTONHOLE BAND

With right side facing and size 2 (2¼ mm) needles and C, pick up and k 131 sts up right front edge.

**Rows 1–3** work in k1 p1 rib, then make buttonholes.

**Row 4** rib 3, bind off 5 sts, *rib 19 (including st on needle), bind off 5 sts; rep from * to last 3 sts, rib 3.

**Row 5** cont in k1 p1 rib, casting on 5 sts over the 6 buttonholes.

**Rows 6 and 7** join on B1 and work in k1 p1 rib.

**Rows 8 and 9** join on A and work in k1 p1 rib.

**Row 10** p (to make foldline).

**Rows 11 and 12** cont in A in k1 p1 rib.

**Rows 13 and 14** join on B1 and work in k1 p1 rib.

**Rows 15 and 16** join on C and work as rows 4 and 5.

**Rows 17–19** work in k1 p1 rib, then bind off loosely in rib. Fold band to inside along foldline and stitch down neatly, neatening around buttonholes using a small buttonhole st.

### BUTTONBAND

With right side facing and size 2 (2¼ mm) needles and C, pick up and k 131 sts down left front. Work 5 rows in k1 p1 rib, then join on B1 and work 2 rows in rib, then join on A and work 2 rows in rib. P next row (to make foldline), then work 2 rows in rib, then join on B1 and work 2 rows in rib, then join on C and work 5 rows in rib, then bind off loosely in rib. Fold band to inside along foldline and stitch down neatly. Sew on buttons.

# RAMBLING ROSES CARDIGAN

Over the years we have planted about a hundred old-fashioned shrub roses in the garden. Their flowering time may be short, but their delicate coloring and delicious scent more than compensate for this. The first pattern, with its blue-and-white background and pink roses, is as subtle as the flowers themselves, and I find the soft colors irresistible. The cardigan is designed to suit infinite colorways, and the second combination is much stronger, with its festive red, green and navy. The ruffles have none of the fussiness of frills. Both patterns are very flattering and feminine, and I have seen both fifteen and eighty year olds looking gorgeous in them.

## MATERIALS

Pair of size 2 (2¼ mm) needles
Set of 4 double-pointed size 2 (2¼ mm) needles
Pair of size 3 (3¼ mm) needles
Set of 4 double-pointed size 3 (3¼ mm) needles
Circular size 3 (3¼ mm) needle 29 in (73.5 cm) long
6 buttons

## WEIGHT OF YARN AND COLORS

**Medium indigo blue (A)**   12 oz (340g)
**Natural (B)**   6 oz (170 g)
**Blue-green (C)**   3 oz (85 g)
**Pale pink (D1)**   3 oz (85 g)
**Pink (D2)**   3 oz (85 g)

## MEASUREMENTS

Length from top of shoulder to bottom edge of cardigan: 21 in (53.5 cm)
Actual width all around at underarm: 46 in (117 cm)
Sleeve length: 22½ in (57 cm)

## GAUGE

Over pattern, using size 3 (3¼ mm) needles (or size to obtain gauge), 30 stitches and 32 rows to 4 in (10 cm)

## IMPORTANT

- This garment is knitted sideways, beginning at left front edge, and the sleeves are also knitted sideways.
- There are two background colors so check that you are using the correct color before beginning each panel: panels 1, 3, 5, 7, and 9 are worked in A and panels 2, 4, 6, and 8 are worked in B.
- Change colors of roses every panel, working pale pink roses on A panels and pink roses on B panels.
- Twist wools at back of work every 1–2 stitches to avoid making holes, but do not pull tight.
- When working St st using just one color, twist a spare ball of the same color yarn across the back of work to keep the thickness of the garment even.

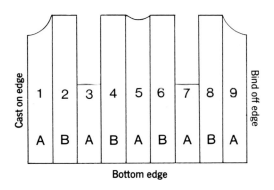

Bottom edge

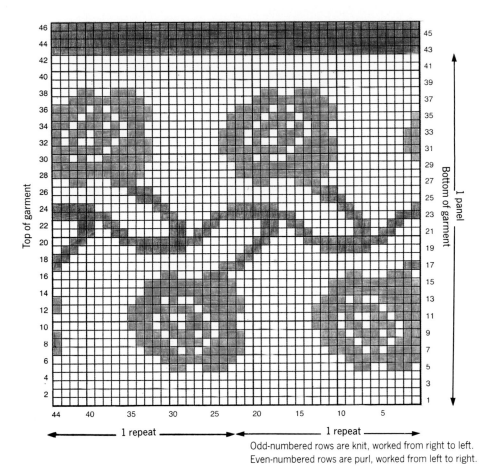

Odd-numbered rows are knit, worked from right to left.
Even-numbered rows are purl, worked from left to right.

## INSTRUCTIONS
### FRONTS AND BACK
#### Panel 1

With size 3 (3¼ mm) needles and A, cast on 104 sts. K 1 row, p 1 row then work next 6 rows as chart, beg at st 1, row 21. Cont working from chart and, beginning with a right side row, shape alternate rows for neck as follows:

**Rows 27 and 29** inc 1 st at end (neck edge) of row.
**Rows 31 and 33** cast on 2 sts at end (neck edge) of row.
**Rows 35 and 37** cast on 3 sts at end (neck edge) of row.
**Rows 39 and 41** cast on 5 sts at end (neck edge) of row.
**Row 42** as chart (126 sts), then work 4 rows rev St st in A as follows:
**Row 1** k.
**Row 2** k.
**Row 3** p.
**Row 4** k.

#### Panel 2

Join on B.
**Rows 1–41** as chart.
**Row 42** With wrong side facing, bind off 52 sts (neck edge), patt to end, then join on A and work 4 rows rev St st as before.

#### Panel 3 (underarm panel)

Cont in A.
**Rows 1–42** as chart, then work 4 rows rev St st as before.

#### Panel 4

Join on B.
**Row 1** patt to end of row (neck edge) and cast on 52 sts.
**Rows 2–42** as chart, then join on A and work 4 rows rev St st as before.

#### Panel 5

Cont in A.
**Rows 1–13** dec 1 st at end (neck edge) of 1st and every following 4th row (122 sts).
**Rows 14–29** as chart.
**Rows 30–42** inc 1 st at beg (neck edge) of 30th and every following 4th row (126 sts), then work 4 rows rev St st as before.

#### Panel 6

Join on B.
**Rows 1–41** as chart.
**Row 42** bind off 52 sts (neck edge), patt to end (74 sts), then join on A and work 4 rows rev St st as before.

#### Panel 7 (underarm panel)

Cont in A.
**Rows 1–42** as chart, then work 4 rows rev St st as before.

#### Panel 8

Join on B.
**Row 1** Patt to end of row (neck edge) and cast on 52 sts.
**Rows 2–42** as chart, then join on A and work 4 rows rev St st as before.

#### Panel 9

Cont in A.
**Row 1** as chart, then cont working from chart, dec alternate rows as follows:
**Rows 2 and 4** bind off 5 sts (neck edge), then patt to end.
**Rows 6 and 8** bind off 3 sts (neck edge), then patt to end.
**Rows 10 and 12** bind off 2 sts (neck edge), then patt to end.
**Rows 14 and 16** bind off 1 st (neck edge), then patt to end.
**Rows 17–22** as chart (104 sts). With A, k 1 row, p 1 row then bind off loosely. Weave in any loose ends using

**Next round** p, then bind off loosely knitwise.

**Frill 2** With set of 4 double-pointed size 2 (2¼ mm) needles and A, pick up and k 50 sts along round indicated by marker on inside of cuff. Work 3 rounds in k1 p1 rib, then loop a short strand of brightly colored wool round 1st st. Work 2 more rounds in k1 p1 rib, then change to set of 4 double-pointed size 3 (3¼ mm) needles and work 1 round, inc into every st (100 sts). Join on D.

**Next round** work in k1 p1 rib.

**Next round** p, then bind off loosely knitwise.

**Frill 3** With set of 4 double-pointed size 2 (2¼ mm) needles and A, pick up and k 50 sts around line indicated by 2nd marker on inside of cuff. Work 5 rounds in k1 p1 rib, then change to set of 4 double-pointed size 3 (3¼ mm) needles and work 1 round, inc into every st (100 sts).

**Next round** k1 p1 to end.

**Next round** p, then bind off loosely knitwise.

### WELT

With right side facing and 2¼ mm (size 3) needles and A, pick up and k 230 sts along lower edge of fronts and back. Work 25 rows in k1 p1 rib. Loop short strand brightly colored wool round 1st and last st as markers. Work 2 more rows in k1 p1 rib.

**Frill 1** Change to size 3 (3¼ mm) needles and work 1 row, inc into every st (460 sts). (Tip: slip sts onto size 3 (3¼ mm) circular needle as this will accommodate all the sts more comfortably and just k from it lengthwise.) Join on C.

**Next row** work in k1 p1 rib.

**Next row** k, then bind off loosely purlwise.

**Frill 2** With size 2 (2¼ mm) needles and A, pick up and k 230 sts along row indicated by markers on inside of welt and work 3 rows in k1 p1 rib. Loop a short strand of brightly colored wool around 1st and last st as markers. Work 2 more rows in k1 p1 rib. Change to size 3 (3¼ mm) needles (or circular needle as before) and work 1 row, inc into every st (460 sts). Join on D.

**Next row** work in k1 p1 rib.

**Next row** k, then bind off loosely purlwise.

**Frill 3** With size 2 (2¼ mm) needles and A, pick up and k 230 sts along row indicated by 2nd markers on inside of welt. Work 5 rows in k1 p1 rib, then change to size 3 (3¼ mm) needles (or circular needle as before) and work 1 row, inc into every st (460 sts).

**Next row** work in k1 p1 rib.

**Next row** k, then bind off loosely purlwise.

### NECKBAND

With right side facing and size 2 (2¼ mm) needles and A, pick up and k 110 sts around neck. Work 5 rows in k1 p1 rib.

**Frill 1** Change to size 3 (3¼ mm) needles and work 1 row, inc into every st to end, then pick up and k 4 sts down side of ribbing (224 sts). Join on C.

**Next row** work in k1 p1 rib to end, then pick up and k 4 sts down side of ribbing (228 sts), then k 2 more rows

---

a darning needle (do not just cut them off). Block (see page 155) garment and press carefully on wrong side using a damp cloth.

### SHOULDER SEAMS

With right side facing and 2¼ mm (size 3) needles and A, pick up and k 40 sts along right front shoulder. K 1 row, p 1 row and k 1 row. Leave sts on spare needle. With 2¼ mm (size 3) needles and A, pick up and k 40 sts along right back shoulder and leave sts on needle. Graft (see page 000) right front shoulder to right back shoulder (right sides together). Rep for left shoulder.

### SLEEVES

With size 3 (3¼ mm) needles and A, cast on 133 sts. Work 4 complete panels from chart in order A, B, A, B, with 4 rows rev St st in A between each panel and end with 4 rows rev St st in A. Leave sts on needle, then press carefully on wrong side using a damp cloth. Graft

---

(see page 155) sts on needle to sts of cast on edge (right sides together). Weave in any loose ends using a darning needle (do not just cut them off). Rep for 2nd sleeve.

### Cuffs

With set of 4 double-pointed size 2 (2¼ mm) needles and A, pick up and k 122 sts along lower edge of sleeve (right side facing, ensuring patt is right way up, that is, with roses growing up toward shoulder).

**Dec round 1** *k2 tog; rep from * around (61 sts).

**Dec round 2** *k4, k2 tog; rep from * to last 7 sts, k4, k3 tog (50 sts), then work 24 more rounds in k1 p1 rib. Loop a short strand of brightly colored wool around 1st st as marker and then work 2 more rounds in k1 p1 rib.

**Frill 1** Change to set of 4 double-pointed size 3 (3¼ mm) needles and work 1 round, inc into every st (100 sts), then join on C.

**Next round** work in k1 p1 rib.

and bind off loosely purlwise.

**Frill 2** Turn frill 1 down onto right side of work and with size 2 (2¼ mm) needles and A, pick up and k 110 sts on inside of neckband in exactly the same place as for frill 1. Work 7 rows in k1 p1 rib, then change to size 3 (3¼ mm) needles and work 1 row, inc into every st to end, then pick up and k 6 sts down side of ribbing (226 sts). Join on D.

**Next row** work in k1 p1 rib to end and pick up and k 6 sts down side of ribbing (232 sts), then k 2 more rows and bind off loosely purlwise.

**Frill 3** Turn frills 1 and 2 down onto right side of work and with size 2 (2¼ mm) needles and A, pick up and k 110 sts on inside of neckband in exactly the same place as for frills 1 and 2. Work 11 rows in k1 p1 rib, then change to size 3 (3¼ mm) needles and work 1 row, inc into every st to end, then pick up and k 10 sts down side of ribbing (230 sts).

**Next row** work in k1 p1 rib to end and pick up and k 10 sts down side of ribbing (240 sts), then k 2 more rows and bind off loosely purlwise.

## BUTTONHOLE BAND

With right side facing and size 2 (2¼ mm) needles and A, pick up and k 127 sts up right front edge.

**Rows 1–3** work in k1 p1 rib, then make buttonholes.

**Row 4** rib 3, bind off 6, *rib 17 (including st on needle), bind off 6; rep from * to last 3 sts, rib 3.

**Row 5** cont in k1 p1 rib, casting on 6 sts over the 6 buttonholes.

**Rows 6–9** work in k1 p1 rib.

**Row 10** p (to make foldline).

**Rows 11–14** work in k1 p1 rib.

**Rows 15 and 16** as rows 4 and 5.

**Rows 17–19** rows in k1 p1 rib, then bind off loosely in rib. Fold band to inside along foldline and stitch down neatly, neatening around buttonholes using a small buttonhole st.

## BUTTON BAND

With right side facing and size 2 (2¼ mm) needles and A, pick up and k 127 sts down left front edge. Work 9 rows in k1 p1 rib, p next row (to make foldline), work 9 more rows in k1 p1 rib, then bind off loosely in rib. Fold band to inside along foldline and stitch down neatly. Sew on buttons.

## SLEEVE INSERTION

With right side facing and set of 4 double-pointed size 2 (2¼ mm) needles and A, pick up and k 132 sts around top edge of sleeve. Work 3 rounds in p, then cast off loosely purlwise. Rep for 2nd sleeve. Place sleeves in armholes with right sides tog, matching underarm panels. Sew neat seams using small back sts.

## FINISHING

Weave in any loose ends using a darning needle. Press carefully on wrong side using a damp cloth, but do not press ribbing or frills.

# FLORAL BAND

## MATERIALS

Short circular size 5 (4½ mm) needle
Size G (3 mm) crochet hook
Approximately 2 ft by 2½ in (60 by 6 cm) strip of 4 oz (115 g) polyester padding

## WEIGHT OF YARN AND COLORS

**PLIED YARN**    (or 2 strands of ordinary yarn knitted together)
**Navy (A)**    3 oz (85 g)
**UNPLIED YARN**    (for flowers)
½ oz (14 g) each of 5 colors (**B**)

## GAUGE

Over stockinette stitch, using circular size 5 (4½ mm) needle (or size to obtain gauge), 25 stitches and 24 rows to 4 in (10 cm).

## IMPORTANT

● The band is knitted on a circular needle so every round is knit.

## INSTRUCTIONS

### BAND

With size 5 (4½ mm) circular needle and A, cast on 100 sts. Work 40 rounds in St st, then bind off loosely. Weave in any loose ends using a darning needle (do not just cut them off), then press on wrong side using a damp cloth.

## FINISHING

### Band

Lay band (wrong side up) on a flat surface and lay the strip of padding down the center. Bring each side of band up over padding to meet along center and oversew edges neatly in A.

### Flower

(See page 157 for Crochet instructions.)

*With size G (3 mm) crochet hook and B, work 9 ch and join into a circle by working a sl st through 1st ch.

**Round 1** work 6 ch, *1 double crochet into circle, 3 ch; rep from * 4 times more, then join into a circle by working a sl st through 3rd of 1st 6 ch (forming 6 loops).

**Round 2** *work 1 single crochet, 1 half-double, 3 doubles, 1 half-double, 1 single crochet into 1st loop; rep from * for rem 5 loops, then join into a circle by working a sl st through 1st single crochet and cut off wool.

**Round 3** rejoin wool at back of work, looping it into top of double of round 1, * work 5 ch, 1 single crochet in top of next double of round 1; rep from * 4 more times, work 5 ch, then join to 1st sl st to complete round 1.

**Round 4** *work 1 single crochet, 1 half-double, 5 doubles, 1 half-double, 1 single crochet into 1st loop; rep from * for rem 5 loops. Fasten off. Weave in any loose ends using a darning needle (do not just cut them off).

Rep from *, making 2 flowers in each color wool. Stitch to band at junctions of petals using matching color and leaving equal spaces between them.

# RIBBONS AND BOWS COAT

This is a simple if large piece of knitting, and the dyeing of the base colors is straightforward. The navy can be dyed in one go by multiplying the recipe by five. Dye the indigo in one batch too so that it all matches. Shade the bows with the four reds in as many different combinations as you like, and the bows will take on a three-dimensional life of their own. I have to confess that this design was originally an error. It turned out longer than intended, so I reworked it to transform it into a coat.

## MATERIALS

Pair of size 2 (2¼ mm) needles
Set of 4 double-pointed size 2 (2¼ mm) needles
2 pairs of size 3 (3¼ mm) needles
Circular size 3 (3¼ mm) needle 29 in (73.5 cm) long
2 stitch holders
12 buttons

## WEIGHT OF YARN AND COLORS

Navy (A)    20 oz (560 g)
Dark indigo blue (B)    12 oz (340 g)
Redwood pink (C1)    4 oz (115 g)
Red (C2)    4 oz (115 g)
Crimson (C3)    4 oz (115 g)
Magenta (C4)    4 oz (115 g)

## MEASUREMENTS

Length from top of shoulder to bottom edge of coat:
40½ in (103 cm)
Actual width all around at underarm: 54 in (137 cm)
Sleeve length: 19½ in (50 cm)

## TENSION

Over pattern, using size 3 (3¼ mm) needles (or size to obtain gauge), 32 stitches and 34 rows to 4 in (10 cm).

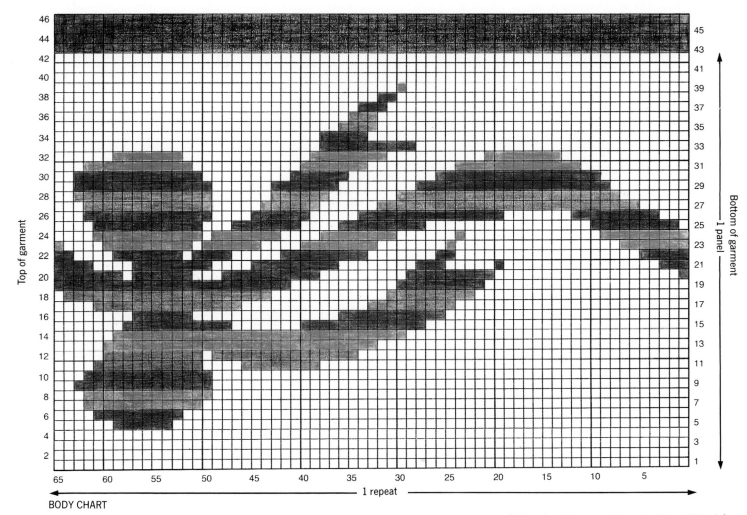

**BODY CHART**

Odd-numbered rows are knit, worked from right to left.
Even-numbered rows are purl, worked from left to right.

## IMPORTANT

- Change shade of red of pattern every 2–3 rows to give a random effect.
- Twist wools at back of work every 1–2 stitches to avoid making holes, but do not pull tight.
- When working St st using just one color, twist a spare ball of the same color yarn across the back of work to keep the thickness of the garment even.
- This garment is knitted sideways, beginning at the left front edge and the sleeves are knitted from cuff to shoulder.
- There are 2 background colors so always check that you are using the correct color: panels 1, 3, 5, 7, and 9 are in A and panels 2, 4, 6, 8, and 10 are in B.
- The pattern on the fronts and back is staggered; therefore begin panels 1, 3, 5, 7, and 9 at stitch 26, row 1 of the Body chart and panels 2, 4, 6, 8, and 10 at stitch 1, row 1 of the chart.
- The pattern on the sleeves is also staggered; therefore begin panels 1 and 3 at stitch 1, row 1 of the Sleeve chart and panel 2 at stitch 38, row 1.

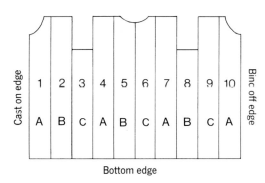

## INSTRUCTIONS
### FRONTS AND BACK
#### Panel 1

With size 3 (3¼ mm) needles and A, cast on 257 sts and work from Body chart, beg at st 26, row 1.
**Rows 1–12** as chart.
**Rows 13–19** inc 1 st at end (neck edge) of this and next 3 alternate rows.

**Rows 20–23** inc 1 st at end (neck edge) of each row (265 sts).
**Row 24** cast on 15 sts, patt to end (280 sts).
**Rows 25–42** as chart, then work 4 rows rev St st in A as follows:
**Row 1** k.
**Row 2** k.
**Row 3** p.
**Row 4** k.

#### Panel 2

Join on B. Work from Body chart, beg at st 1, row 1.
**Rows 1–41** as chart.
**Pocket lining** Set work on one side and with size 3 (3¼ mm) needles and B, cast on 42 sts and work 41 rows St st. Keep sts on needle. Return to main body of work and cont as follows:
**Row 42** bind off 60 sts, patt 78 sts. Slip next 42 sts onto a st holder for pocket, then join on pocket lining, p from its needle, keeping to patt, and patt to end (220 sts). Then join on A and work 4 rows rev St st as before.

# 120 RIBBONS AND BOWS

Top of garment

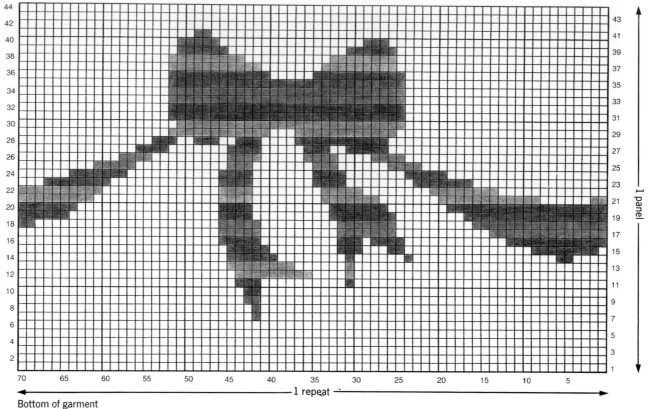

Bottom of garment
SLEEVE CHART

Odd-numbered rows are knit, worked from right to left.
Even-numbered rows are purl, worked from left to right.

**Panel 3** (underarm panel)
Cont in A. Work from Body chart, beg at st 26, row 1.
**Rows 1–42** as chart, then work 4 rows rev St st as before.

**Panel 4**
Join on B. Work from Body chart, beg at st 1, row 1.
**Row 1** patt to end, cast on 60 sts (280 sts).
**Rows 2–42** as chart, then join on A and work 4 rows rev St st as before.

**Panel 5**
Cont in A. Work from Body chart, beg at st 26, row 1.
**Rows 1–18** as chart.
**Rows 19–23** dec 1 st at end (neck edge) of row 19 and next 2 alternate rows (277 sts).
**Rows 24–42** as chart, then work 4 rows rev St st as before.

**Panel 6**
Join on B and work from Body chart, beg at st 1, row 1.
**Rows 1–18** as chart.
**Rows 19–23** inc 1 st at end (neck edge) of this and next 2 alternate rows (280 sts).
**Rows 24–42** as chart, then join on A and work 4 rows rev St st as before.

**Panel 7**
Cont in A. Work from Body chart, beg at st 26, row 1.
**Rows 1–41** as chart.
**Row 42** bind off 60 sts, patt to end (220 sts), then work 4 rows rev St st as before.

**Panel 8** (underarm panel)
Join on B. Work from Body chart, beg at st 1, row 1.
**Rows 1–42** as chart.
**Pocket top** Lay work aside and with size 2 (2¼ mm) needles and A, cast on 42 sts and work 10 rows in k1 p1 rib. P next row (to make foldline), then work 9 more rows in k1 p1 rib. Keep sts on spare needle. Return to main body of work, cont as follows:
**1st row of rev St st** join on A and k 100 sts. Slip sts of pocket top onto needle and k them. Slip next 42 sts onto a st holder, then k to end. Complete panel of rev St st (k this row, p next row, k last row).

**Panel 9**
Cont in A. Work from Body chart, beg at st 26, row 1.
**Row 1** patt to end, then cast on 60 sts (280 sts).
**Rows 2–42** as chart, then work 4 rows rev St st as before.

**Panel 10**
Join on B. Work from Body chart, beg at st 1, row 1.

**Rows 1–19** as chart.
**Row 20** bind off 15 sts (neck edge) and patt to end (265 sts).
**Rows 21–24** dec 1st at neck edge of each row.
**Rows 25–31** dec 1 st at end (neck edge) of this and next 3 alternate rows (257 sts).
**Rows 32–42** as chart, then bind off loosely.

**Finishing pockets**
**Left pocket top** With wrong side facing and size 3 (3¼ mm) needles and B, slip the 42 sts from st holder onto needle and p them, then join on A and work 4 rows rev St st as before. Change to size 2 (2¼ mm) needles and work 9 rows in k1 p1 rib. K next row (to make foldline), work 9 more rows in k1 p1 rib, then bind off loosely in rib.
**Right pocket lining** With right side facing and size 3 (3¼ mm) needles and A, slip sts from st holder onto needle and complete border of rev St st (k next 2 rows, p next and k last row). Cont with A and work 42 rows St st. Bind off loosely.
Block (see page 155) garment and press carefully on wrong side using a damp cloth, but do not press ribbing. Stitch pocket linings in place carefully. Fold pocket tops to inside along foldline and stitch down neatly. Weave in any loose ends using a darning needle (do not just cut them off).

### Shoulder seams

With size 2 (2¼ mm) needles and A, pick up and k 60 sts along right front shoulder (right side facing). Work 3 rows rev St st.

**Row 1** k.
**Row 2** p.
**Row 3** k.

Leave sts on a spare needle.

With right side facing and size 2 (2¼ mm) needles and A, pick up and k 60 sts along right back shoulder. Leave sts on needle. Graft (see page 155) right front shoulder to right back shoulder (right sides together). Rep for left shoulder.

### SLEEVES

#### Right sleeve

With set of 4 double-pointed size 2 (2¼ mm) needles and A, cast on 60 sts and work 36 rounds in k1 p1 rib.
**Next round** p (to make foldline), then work 36 more rounds in k1, p1 rib.
**Inc round 1** *k1, inc into next st; rep from * to end (90 sts).
**Inc round 2** inc into every st (180 sts).
**Inc round 3** *k5, inc into next st; rep from * to end (210 sts).

#### Panel 1

Change to circular size 3 (3¼ mm) needle, join on B, and work from Sleeve chart, beg at st 1, round 1.
**Rounds 1–42** as chart, then join on A and work 4 rounds rev St st as follows: round 1 k; round 2 p; round 3 p; round 4 p.

#### Panel 2

Cont in A, beg patt at st 38, round 1 of Sleeve chart.
**Rounds 1–42** as chart, then work 4 rows rev St st as before.

#### Panel 3

Join on B and work from Sleeve chart, beg at st 1, round 1.
**Rounds 1–41** as chart.
**Round 42** *k3, k2 tog; rep from * to end (168 sts), then join on A and work 4 rows rev St st as before. Bind off loosely.

#### Left sleeve

Work as right sleeve, but rev colors, i.e., work panel 1 in A, panel 2 in B, and panel 3 in A.

### WELT

With right side facing and size 2 (2¼ mm) needles and A, pick up and k 400 sts around bottom edge of fronts and back. Work 36 rows in k1 p1 rib.
**Next row** k (to make foldline), then work 36 more rows in k1 p1 rib. Bind off loosely in rib. Fold welt to inside along foldline and stitch down neatly.

### NECKBAND

With right side facing and size 2 (2¼ mm) needles and A, pick up and k 100 sts around neck. Work 9 rows in k1 p1 rib. P next row (to make foldline), then work 9 more rows in k1 p1 rib. Bind off loosely in rib. Fold band to inside along foldline and stitch down neatly.

### BUTTONHOLE BAND

With right side facing and size 2 (2¼ mm) needles and A, pick up and k 298 sts up right front edge.
**Rows 1–4** work in k1 p1 rib, then make buttonholes:
**Row 5** rib 3, bind off 6 sts, *rib 20 (counting stitch already on needle), bind off 6 sts; rep from * to last 3 sts, rib 3.
**Row 6** cont in k1 p1 rib, casting on 6 sts over the 12 buttonholes.
**Rows 7–9** work in k1 p1 rib.
**Row 10** p (to make foldline).
**Rows 11–13** work in k1 p1 rib.
**Rows 14 and 15** as rows 5 and 6.
**Rows 16–19** work in k1 p1 rib, then bind off loosely in rib. Fold band to inside along foldline and stitch down neatly, neatening around buttonholes with a small buttonhole st.

### BUTTON BAND

With right side facing and size 2 (2¼ mm) needles and A, pick up and k 298 sts down left front edge. Work 9 rows in k1 p1 rib, p next row (to make foldline), work 9 more rows in k1 p1 rib, then bind off loosely in rib. Fold to inside along foldline and stitch down. Sew on buttons.

### SLEEVE INSERTION

Press carefully on wrong side using a damp cloth, but do not press ribbing. Place sleeve in armhole with right sides tog, ensuring that center of bow is at shoulder seam. Sew neat seam using small back sts. Weave in any loose ends using a darning needle. Fold each cuff to inside along foldline and stitch down neatly.

---

# RUFFLED BAND

## MATERIALS

Pair of size 3 (3¼ mm) needles
Pair of size 5 (4½ mm) needles
Approximately 3 ft 4 in by 4 in (100 by 10 cm) strip of 4 oz (115 g) polyester padding

## WEIGHT OF YARN AND COLORS

**PLIED YARN** (or 2 strands of ordinary yarn knitted together)
**Navy (A)** 4 oz (115 g)
**UNPLIED YARN** (for frills)
**Reds (B)** ½ oz (14 g)
**Medium indigo blue (C)** ½ oz (14 g)
**Navy (D)** ½ oz (14 g)

## GAUGE

Over stockinette stitch, using size 5 (4½ mm) needles, 25 stitches and 24 rows to 4 in (10 cm).

## INSTRUCTIONS

### BAND

With size 5 (4½ mm) needles and A, cast on 100 sts.
**Rows 1–16** work in St st.
**Row 17** k, looping short strands of B at each end of row as markers.
**Rows 18–22** work in St st.
**Row 23** k, looping short strands of D at each end of row as markers.
**Rows 24–28** work in St st.
**Row 29** k, looping short strands of C at each end of row as markers.
**Rows 30–34** work in St st.
**Row 35** k, looping short strands of B at each end of row as markers.
**Rows 36–40** work in St st.
**Row 41** k, looping short strands of D at each end of row as markers.
**Rows 42–46** work in St st.
**Row 47** k, looping short strands of C at each end of row as markers.
**Rows 48–64** work in St st, then bind off loosely. Weave in any loose ends using a darning needle (do not just cut them off) and press carefully on wrong side using a damp cloth.

### FRILLS

With right side facing and size 3 (3¼ mm) needles and B, pick up and k 100 sts along row indicated by 1st markers in B.
**Row 1** p.
**Row 2** k, inc into every st (200 sts).
**Rows 3–6** work in St st, then bind off loosely purlwise. Rep, working a frill along each row indicated by markers in same color wool as markers.

### FINISHING

Lay band (wrong side up) on a flat surface and lay strip of padding down the center. Bring each side of band up over padding to meet along center and oversew edges neatly in A. Then bring ends of band tog to form a circle and stitch ends of padding tog, then oversew edges of ends of band tog. To neaten, stitch edges of ends of each frill tog using very small stitches.

# FIREWORKS JACKET

Names like "bright busters", "Prince of Wales plumes", "flying dragons" and "devil among the tailors" were given to old English fireworks that are no longer made. Interestingly, two of the four have a reference to clothing, and for me this design is an attempt to make a jacket look like a firework's display. I studied the patterns they made, then tried to translate it onto paper without losing the sense of explosion and movement. The end result is fun to knit because the patterning uses plenty of colors and leaves the knitter free to vary the combinations. The red, pink, and elderberry background is unusual, and looks awful in anything but natural dyes. The ribs are picked up after the main bulk of the knitting has been completed. If it is properly woven, the patterning should be visible from the inside as well as the outside.

## MATERIALS
Pair of size 2 (2¼ mm) needles
Set of 4 double-pointed size 2 (2¼ mm) needles
2 pairs of size 3 (3¼ mm) needles
2 stitch holders
7 buttons

## WEIGHT OF YARN AND COLORS
Red (A)   8 oz (230 g)
Elderberry (B)   10 oz (280 g)
Pink (C)   6 oz (170 g)
Walnut (D1)   2 oz (57 g)
Pale walnut (D2)   2 oz (57 g)
Gray (D3)   2 oz (57 g)
Natural (D4)   2 oz (57 g)
Grape (D5)   2 oz (57 g)

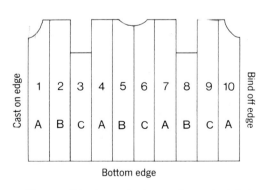

Odd-numbered rows are knit, worked from right to left.
Even-numbered rows are purl, worked from left to right.

## MEASUREMENTS

Length from top of shoulder to bottom edge of jacket:
32½ in (82.5 cm)
Actual width all around at underarm: 56 in (142 cm)
Sleeve length: 23½ in (60 cm)

## GAUGE

Over pattern, using size 3 (3¼ mm) needles (or size to
obtain gauge), 28 stitches and 30 rows to 4 in (10 cm).

## IMPORTANT

• Change colors of firework motif every 2–3 rows to
give a random effect, using D shades.
• Twist wools at back of work every 2–3 sts to avoid
making holes, but do not pull tight.
• When working St st using just one color, twist a
spare ball of the same color yarn across the back of
work to keep the thickness of the garment even.
• This garment is knitted sideways, beginning at left
front edge, and the sleeves are also knitted sideways.

| Cast on edge | 1 | 2 | 3 | 4 | 5 | 6 | 7 | 8 | 9 | 10 | Bind off edge |
|---|---|---|---|---|---|---|---|---|---|---|---|
|  | A | B | C | A | B | C | A | B | C | A |  |

Bottom edge

• There are 3 background colors so always check that
you are using the correct color: panels 1, 4, 7, and 10
are in A, panels 2, 5, and 8 are in B and panels 3, 6,
and 9 are in C.
• The pattern throughout is staggered, so begin panels
1, 3, 5, 7, and 9 at stitch 1 of the chart and panels 2, 4,
6, 8, and 10 at stitch 41.

## INSTRUCTIONS
### FRONTS AND BACK

**Panel 1**
With size 3 (3¼ mm) needles and A, cast on 172 sts
and work from chart, beg at st 1, row 1.
**Rows 1–12** as chart.
**Rows 13** With right side facing inc 1 st at end (neck
edge) of row.
**Rows 14–16** as chart.
**Rows 17–29** inc 1 st at end (neck edge) of 17th row
and next 6 alternate rows.
**Rows 30 and 31** as chart.
**Row 32** With wrong side facing cast on 15 sts, patt to
end (195 sts).
**Rows 33–42** as chart, then join on B and work 4 rows
rev st st as follows:
**Row 1** k.
**Row 2** k.
**Row 3** p.
**Row 4** k.

## Panel 2

Cont in B and work from chart, beg at st 41, row 1 of chart.

**Rows 1–41** as chart.

**Row 42** Bind off 52 sts (for armhole), patt to end (143 sts). Work 4 rows rev st st as before.

**Pocket lining** Lay work aside and with 2nd pair of size 3 (3¼ mm) needles and B, cast on 42 sts and work rows 1–42 of chart, beg at st 65, row 1. Keep sts on needle.

Return to main body of work and cont as follows:

## Panel 3 (underarm panel)

Join on C and work from chart, beg at st 1, row 1.

**Row 1** Patt 24, slip next 42 sts onto a st holder. Join on pocket lining, k from its needle, then patt to end.

**Rows 1–42** as chart, then join on B and work 4 rows rev St st as before.

## Panel 4

Join on A and work from chart, beg at st 41, row 1.

**Row 1** With right side facing patt to end, then cast on 52 sts (195 sts).

**Rows 2–42** as chart, then join on B and work 4 rows rev St st as before.

## Panel 5

Cont in B and work from chart, beg at st 1, row 1.

**Rows 1–10** as chart.

**Rows 11–15** dec 1 st at end (neck edge) of 11th row and next 2 alternate rows (192 sts).

**Rows 16–42** as chart, then work 4 rows rev St st as before.

## Panel 6

Join on C and work from chart, beg at st 41, row 1.

**Rows 1–26** as chart.

**Rows 27–31** inc 1 st at end (neck edge) of 27th row and next 2 alternate rows (195 sts).

**Rows 32–42** as chart, then join on B and work 4 rows rev St st as before.

## Panel 7

Join on A and work from chart, beg at st 1, row 1.

**Rows 1–41** as chart.

**Row 42** With wrong side facing bind off 52 sts, patt to end (143 sts), then join on B and work 4 rows rev St st as before.

## Panel 8 (underarm panel)

Cont in B and work from chart, beg at st 41, row 1.

**Rows 1–42** as chart.

**Pocket top** Lay work aside and with size 2 (2¼ mm) needles and B, cast on 42 sts and work 6 rows in k1 p1 rib.

Keep sts on a spare needle.

Return to main body of work and cont as follows:

**1st row of rev St st** cont in B and k 24 sts. Slip sts of pocket top onto needle and k them. Slip next 42 sts

onto a st holder, then k to end. Complete panel of rev St st (k this row, p next row, k last row).

## Panel 9

Join on C and work from chart, beg at st 1, row 1.

**Row 1** With right side facing patt to end, then cast on 52 sts (195 sts).

**Rows 2–42** as chart, then join on B and work 4 rows rev St st as before.

## Panel 10

Join on A and work from chart, beg at st 41, row 1.

**Rows 1–11** as chart.

**Row 12** With wrong side facing bind off 15 sts (neck edge), patt to end (180 sts).

**Rows 13 and 14** as chart.

**Rows 15–27** dec 1 st at end (neck edge) of row 15 and next 6 alternate rows (173 sts).

**Rows 28–30** as chart.

**Row 31** dec 1 st at end (neck edge) of row (172 sts).

**Rows 32–42** as chart, then bind off loosely.

## Finishing pockets

**Left pocket top** With right side facing and size 2 (2¼ mm) needles and B, slip the 42 sts from st holder onto needle and work 6 rows in k1 p1 rib, then bind off loosely in rib.

**Right pocket lining** With right side facing and size 3 (3¼ mm) needles and C, slip sts from st holder onto needle, and work from chart, beg at st 25, row 1, working rows 1–42 as chart, then bind off loosely. Block (see page 155) garment and press carefully on wrong side using a damp cloth, but do not press ribbing. Stitch pocket linings and edges of pocket tops in place carefully and weave in any loose ends using a darning needle (do not just cut them off).

## Shoulder seams

With right side facing and size 2 (2¼ mm) needles and B, pick up and k 52 sts along right front shoulder. Work 3 rows rev St st as follows:

**Row 1** k.

**Row 2** p.

**Row 3** k.

Leave sts on a spare needle.

With size 2 (2¼ mm) needles and B, pick up and k 52 sts along right back shoulder (right side facing). Leave sts on needle. Graft (see page 155) right front shoulder to right back shoulder (right sides together). Rep for left shoulder.

## SLEEVES

With size 3 (3¼ mm) needles and A, cast on 123 sts. Work 4 panels from chart in order A, B, C, B, beg at st 1 or 41, row 1 as before, with 4 rows rev St st in B between each panel and end with 4 rows rev St st in B. Leave sts on needle. Graft (see page 155) sts on needle to sts of cast-on edge (right sides together). Weave in any loose ends using a darning needle (do not just cut

them off), then press carefully. Rep for 2nd sleeve.

## Cuffs

With right side facing and set of 4 double-pointed size 2 (2¼ mm) needles and B, pick up and k 160 sts along lower edge of sleeve, making sure patt is right way up.

**Dec round 1** *k2 tog; rep from * around (80 sts).

**Dec round 2** *k2, k2 tog; rep from * around (60 sts), then work 36 more rounds in k1 p1 rib. Join on 2nd strand B and bind off loosely in rib.

## WELT

With right side facing and size 2 (2¼ mm) needles and B, pick up and k 350 sts along lower edge of fronts and back (right side facing). Work 36 rows in k1 p1 rib. Join on 2nd strand B and bind off loosely in rib.

## NECKBAND

With right side facing and size 2 (2¼ mm) needles and B, pick up and k 110 sts around neck. Work 9 rows in k1 p1 rib. P next row (to make foldline), then work 9 more rows in k1 p1 rib and bind off loosely in rib. Fold band to inside along foldline and stitch down neatly.

## BUTTONHOLE BAND

With right side facing and size 2 (2¼ mm) needles and B, pick up and k 218 sts up right front edge.

**Rows 1–4** work in k1 p1 rib, then make buttonholes.

**Row 5** rib 4, bind off 6, *rib 28 (including st on needle), bind off 6; rep from * to last 4 sts, rib 4.

**Row 6** cont in k1 p1 rib, casting on 6 sts over the 7 buttonholes.

**Rows 7–9** work in k1 p1 rib.

**Row 10** p (to make foldline).

**Rows 11–13** work in k1 p1 rib.

**Rows 14 and 15** as rows 5 and 6.

**Rows 16–19** work in k1 p1 rib, then bind off loosely in rib. Fold band to inside along foldline and stitch down neatly, neatening around buttonholes using a small buttonhole st.

## BUTTON BAND

With right side facing and size 2 (2¼ mm) needles and B, pick up and k 218 sts down left front edge. Work 9 rows in k1 p1 rib, p next row (to make foldline), work 9 more rows in k1 p1 rib, then bind off loosely in rib. Fold band to inside along foldline and stitch down neatly. Sew on buttons.

## SLEEVE INSERTION

With right side facing and set of 4 double-pointed size 2 (2¼ mm) needles and B, pick up and k 132 sts around top edge of sleeve. Work 3 rounds in p, then bind off loosely knitwise. Rep for 2nd sleeve.

Place sleeves in armholes with right sides tog, taking care to match underarm panels. Sew neat seams using small back sts. Weave in any rem loose ends using a darning needle (do not just cut them off).

# SUNFLOWER JACKET

When the painter Vincent van Gogh moved to Arles in the south of France in 1888, he immediately painted his house yellow and decorated it with six pictures of sunflowers. To van Gogh, yellow was the color of the sun, the symbol of light and warmth, and he intended his sunflowers to have the effect of a stained-glass window in a medieval church, to glow with and enrich the light. This jacket is my homage to van Gogh, particularly his brave use of color. I have tried to follow his example by using the madder as a background and giving both leaves and flowers the texture of paint, by using several tones of yellow and green. It is vital that you knit the gauge square before embarking on the jacket. Carry the yarns not in use loosely across the back of the knitting by twisting them on every two to three stitches.

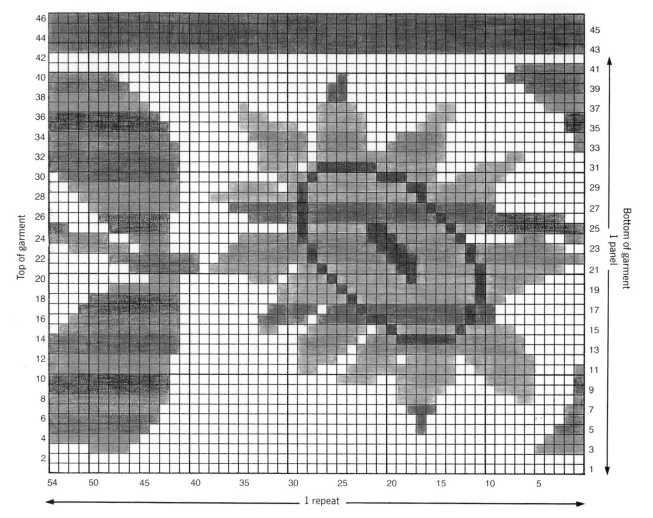

Odd-numbered rows are knit, worked from right to left.          Even-numbered rows are purl, worked from left to right.

## MATERIALS

Pair of size 2 (2¼ mm) needles
Set of 4 double-pointed size 2 (2¼ mm) needles
2 pairs of size 3 (3¼ mm) needles
2 stitch holders
7 buttons

## WEIGHT OF YARN AND COLORS

**Madder (A)**   24 oz (675 g)
**Olive green (B1)**   3 oz (85 g)
**Blue-green (B2)**   3 oz (85 g)
**Grass green (B3)**   3 oz (85 g)
**Primrose (C1)**   2 oz (57 g)
**Yellow (C2)**   2 oz (57 g)
**Buttercup yellow (C3)**   2 oz (57 g)
**Ochre (D)**   2 oz (57 g)

## MEASUREMENTS

Length from top of shoulder to bottom edge of jacket:
30 in (76 cm)
Actual width all around at underarm: 59 in (150 cm)
Sleeve length: 21 in (53 cm)

## GAUGE

Over pattern, using size 3 (3¼ mm) needles (or size to obtain gauge), 28 stitches and 28 rows to 4 in (10 cm).

## IMPORTANT

● Change the yellow of the sunflowers and green of the leaves and stems every 2–3 rows to give a random effect.
● Twist wools at back of work every 2–3 stitches to avoid making holes, but do not pull tight.
● When working St st using just one color, twist a spare ball of the same color yarn across the back of work to keep the thickness of the garment even.
● This garment is knitted sideways, beginning at left front edge, and the sleeves are also knitted sideways.
● The pattern throughout is staggered, so begin panels 1, 3, 5, 7, and 9 at stitch 49 of the chart and panels 2, 4, 6, 8, and 10 at stitch 17.

## INSTRUCTIONS
### FRONTS AND BACK

**Panel 1**

With size 3 (3¼ mm) needles and A, cast on 172 sts and work from chart, beg at st 49, row 1, working sunflowers in shades of C and leaves and stems in shades of B in random numbers of rows. Use D for center and outer ring of flowers.
**Rows 1–12** as chart.
**Row 13** With right side facing inc 1 st at end (neck edge) of row.
**Rows 14–16** as chart.
**Rows 17–29** inc 1 st at end (neck edge) of 17th row and next 6 alternate rows.
**Rows 30 and 31** as chart.
**Row 32** cast on 15 sts, patt to end (195 sts).
**Rows 33–42** as chart, then join on B1 and work 4 rows rev St st as follows:
**Row 1** k.
**Row 2** k.
**Row 3** p.
**Row 4** k.

## Panel 2

Join on A and work from chart, beg at st 17, row 1.
**Rows 1–41** as chart.
**Row 42** Bind off 52 sts, patt to end (143 sts). Work 4 rows rev St st as before.
**Pocket lining** Lay work aside and with 2nd pair of size 3 (3¼ mm) needles and A, cast on 42 sts and work rows 1–42 of chart, beg at st 38, row 1. Keep sts on needle.
Return to main body of work and cont as follows.

## Panel 3 (underarm panel)

Join on A and work from chart, beg at st 49, row 1.
**Row 1** Patt 24, slip next 42 sts onto a st holder, then join on pocket lining, k from its needle, and patt to end.
**Rows 2–42** as chart, then join on B1 and work 4 rows rev St st as before.

## Panel 4

Join on A and work from chart, beg at st 17, row 1.
**Row 1** With right side facing patt to end, then cast on 52 sts (195 sts).
**Rows 2–42** as chart, then join on B1 and work 4 rows rev St st as before.

## Panel 5

Join on A and work from chart, beg at st 19, row 1.
**Rows 1–10** as chart.
**Rows 11–15** dec 1 st at end (neck edge) of 11th row and next 2 alternate rows (192 sts).
**Rows 16–42** as chart, then join on B1 and work 4 rows rev St st as before.

## Panel 6

Join on A and work from chart, beg at st 17, row 1.
**Rows 1–26** as chart.
**Rows 27–31** inc 1 st at end (neck edge) of 27th row and next 2 alternate rows (195 sts).
**Rows 32–42** as chart, then join on B1 and work 4 rows rev St st as before.

## Panel 7

Join on A and work from chart, beg at st 49, row 1.
**Rows 1–41** as chart.
**Row 42** With wrong side facing bind off 52 sts, patt to end (143 sts), then join on B1 and work 4 rows rev St st as before.

## Panel 8 (underarm panel)

Join on A and work from chart, beg at st 17, row 1.
**Rows 1–42** as chart.
**Pocket top** Lay work aside and with size 2 (2¼ mm) needles and B1, cast on 42 sts and work 2 rows in k1 p1 rib, join on A and work 4 more rows in rib. Keep sts on spare needle. Return to main body of work and cont as follows:
**1st row of rev St st** join on B1 and k 24 sts. Slip sts of pocket top onto needle and k them. Slip next 42 sts onto a st holder, then k to end. Complete panel of rev St st (k this row, p next, k last row).

## Panel 9

Join on A and work from chart, beg at st 49, row 1.
**Row 1** With right side facing, patt to end, then cast on 52 sts (195 sts).
**Rows 2–42** as chart, then join on B and work 4 rows rev St st as before.

## Panel 10

Join on A and work from chart, beg at st 17, row 1.
**Rows 1–11** as chart.
**Row 12** With wrong side facing, bind off 15 sts (neck edge), patt to end (180 sts).
**Rows 13 and 14** as chart.
**Rows 15–27** dec 1 st at end (neck edge) of 15th row and next 6 alternate rows (173 sts).
**Rows 28–30** as chart.
**Row 31** dec 1 st at end (neck edge) of row (172 sts).
**Rows 32–42** as chart, then bind off loosely.
Weave in any loose ends using a darning needle (do not just cut them off). Block (see page 155) garment and press carefully on wrong side using a damp cloth, but do not press ribbing.

## Finishing pockets

**Right pocket lining** With right side facing and size 3 (3¼ mm) needles and A, slip sts from st holder onto needle, join on A and work from chart, beg at st 17, row 1, working rows 1–42 as chart then bind off loosely.
**Left pocket top** With right side facing and size 2 (2¼ mm) needles and A, slip the 42 sts from st holder onto needle and work 4 rows in k1 p1 rib.
Join on B1 and work 2 rows in rib, then bind off loosely in rib. Stitch pocket linings and edges of pocket tops in place carefully. Weave in any loose ends using a darning needle (do not just cut them off).

## Shoulder seams

With right side facing and size 2 (2¼ mm) needles and B1, pick up and k 52 sts along right front shoulder. Work 3 rows rev St st as follows:
**Row 1** k.
**Row 2** p.
**Row 3** k.
Leave sts on spare needle.
With right side facing and size 2 (2¼ mm) needles and B1, pick up and k 52 sts along right back shoulder. Leave sts on needle. Graft (see page 155) right front shoulder to right back shoulder (right sides together). Rep for left shoulder.

## SLEEVES

With size 3 (3¼ mm) needles and A, cast on 123 sts and work 4 panels from chart, beg at st 49 or 17, row 1 as before, with 4 rows rev St st in B1 between each panel and end with 4 rows rev St st in B1. Leave sts on needle. Press carefully on wrong side using a damp cloth. Graft (see page 155) sts on needle to sts of cast-on edge (right sides together). Weave in any loose ends using a darning needle (do not just cut them off). Rep for 2nd sleeve.

## Cuffs

With right side facing and set of 4 double-pointed size 2 (2¼ mm) needles and A, pick up and k 122 sts along lower edge of sleeve, making sure patt is right way up.
**Dec round 1** *k2 tog; rep from * to end (61 sts).
**Dec round 2** *k4, k2 tog; rep from * to last 7 sts, k4, k3 tog (50 sts), then work 36 rounds in k1 p1 rib. Join on B1 and work 2 rounds in k1 p1 rib, join on 2nd strand B1 and bind off loosely in rib.

## WELT

With right side facing and size 2 (2¼ mm) needles and A, pick up and k 350 sts along lower edge of fronts and back. Work 35 rows in k1 p1 rib, join on B1 and work 2 rows in rib, join on 2nd strand B1, then bind off loosely in rib.

## NECKBAND

With right side facing and size 2 (2¼ mm) needles and A, pick up and k 110 sts around neck, beg at right front neck edge. Work 9 rows in k1 p1 rib. P next row (to make foldline), then work 9 more rows in k1 p1 rib and bind off loosely in rib. Fold band to inside along foldline and stitch down neatly.

## BUTTONHOLE BAND

With right side facing and size 2 (2¼ mm) needles and A, pick up and k 218 sts up right front edge.
**Rows 1–4** work in k1 p1 rib, then make buttonholes:
**Row 5** rib 4 sts, bind off 6, *rib 28 (including st on needle), bind off 6; rep from * to last 4 sts, rib 4.
**Row 6** cont in k1 p1 rib, casting on 6 sts over the 7 buttonholes.
**Rows 7–9** work in k1 p1 rib.
**Row 10** p (to make foldline).
**Rows 11–13** work in k1 p1 rib.
**Rows 14 and 15** as rows 5 and 6.
**Rows 16–19** work in k1 p1 rib, then bind off loosely in rib. Fold band to inside along foldline and stitch down neatly, using small buttonhole st around buttonholes.

## BUTTON BAND

With right side facing and size 2 (2¼ mm) needles and A, pick up and k 218 sts down left front edge. Work 9 rows in k1 p1 rib, p next row (to make foldline), work 9 more rows in k1 p1 rib, then bind off loosely in rib. Fold band to inside along foldline and stitch down neatly. Sew on buttons.

## SLEEVE INSERTION

With right side facing and set of 4 double-pointed size 2 (2¼ mm) needles and B1, pick up and k 132 sts around top edge of sleeve. Work 3 rounds in p, then bind off loosely knitwise.
Place sleeves in armholes with right sides tog. Sew neat seams using small back sts. Weave in any rem loose ends using a darning needle (do not just cut them off).

# HIGHWAYMAN JACKET

This jacket marks my most radical departure from traditional Fair Isle design, yet it gives the impression of being a tailored jacket. The highwayman remains a flamboyant figure of legend, and I have given the jacket the huge dramatic sleeves of many of the ballet costumes designed for Diaghilev's **Ballets Russes.** The quality of the knitting is all important, and the tension needs to be perfect if the final jacket is to hang properly.

## MATERIALS

Pair of size 2 (2¼ mm) needles
Set of 4 double-pointed size 2 (2¼ mm) needles
Circular size 2 (2¼ mm) needle 16 in (40 cm) long
Pair of size 3 (3¼ mm) needles
7 stitch holders
8 buttons
8 snap fasteners

## WEIGHT OF YARN AND COLORS

**Natural (A)**    7 oz (200 g)
**Dark gray (B)**    11 oz (310 g)
**Redwood pink (C)**    13 oz (370 g)

## MEASUREMENTS

Length from top of shoulder to bottom edge of jacket: 30 in (76 cm)
Actual width all around at underarm: 38 in (96.5 cm)
Sleeve length: 16½ in (42 cm)

## GAUGE

Over check and moss stitch pattern, using size 3 (3¼ mm) needles (or size to obtain gauge), 32 sts and 36 rows to 4 in (10 cm)

CHART 1
Top of garment

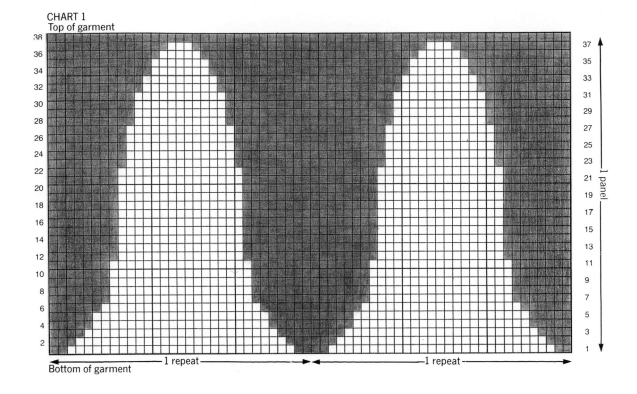

Bottom of garment
1 repeat — 1 repeat
1 panel

## IMPORTANT

• Twist wools at back of work every 1–2 stitches to avoid making holes, but do not pull tight.
• Take care to keep check pattern in 'checkerboard' sequence throughout.
• When you are working in St st using just one color twist a spare ball of the same color yarn across the back of work to keep the thickness of the garment even.
• When changing the yarn color and working in moss st, always knit the first row on the right side to avoid 'color pips.'

## INSTRUCTIONS
### FRONTS AND BACK
#### Peplum

**Right half** **With size 3 (3¼ mm) needles and A, cast on 186 sts and work 6 rows in St st. Join on B and work rows 1–38 as chart 1. With right side facing cont in B only as follows:
**Next row** k14, k3 tog, *k28, k3 tog; rep from * to last 14 sts, k to end (174 sts). Then work 15 more rows in St st, beg with p row.
**Next row** k2, *k2 tog, k15; rep from * to last 2 sts, k2 (164 sts).
**Next row** p. Cut off B, join on C, then k2 tog, k to last 2 sts, k2 tog (162 sts). Then work 7 rows in m st. Cut off C**. Join on A and B and work 12 rows in check patt from chart 2, beg row 1 with k6 in B (right side facing). Cut off A and B. ***Join on 2 strands C, change to size 2 (2¼ mm) needles and cont as follows:
**Next row** *k1, k2 tog; rep from * to end (108 sts).

Work 16 rows in k1 p1 rib.
**Next row** rib 9, *rib 2, inc into next st; rep from * to last 9 sts, rib 9 (138 sts). Cut off both strands C***.
Change back to 3¼ mm (size 10) needles and join on A and B. Keeping checks correct, work 6 rows of check patt from chart 2, inc 1 st at edge of back on every row (i.e., end of rows 1, 3, and 5, and beg of rows 2, 4, and 6; 144 sts). Leave sts on a spare needle.
**Left half** Work as given for right half from ** to **, then cont as follows: work 12 rows check patt from chart 2, beg with k6 in A. Cut off A and B, then work as given for right half from *** to ***. Then change back to size 3 (3¼ mm) needles and, keeping checks correct, work 6 rows of check patt from chart 2, inc 1 st at edge of back on every row (i.e., beg of rows 1, 3, and 5, and end rows 2, 4, and 6; 144 sts). Leave sts on needle.
**Joining 2 halves together** With size 3 (3¼ mm) needles and A and B, keeping checks correct, patt the 144 sts of Right half and then the 144 sts of Left half, making sure that the back edges are tog (288 sts).

#### Waist to armholes

Work 5 rows from chart 2 to complete check patt, then cut off A and B and join on C.
**Next row** k (to avoid color 'pips'). Work 7 rows in m st, then cut off C. Join on A and B and work 12 rows check patt from chart 2, then cut off A and B and join on C. Work 8 rows in m st, then cut off C and join on A and B. Work 12 rows check patt from chart 2, cut off A and B and join on C. Work 8 rows in m st, then cut off C.

Odd-numbered rows are knit, worked from right to left (except the moss st panel).
Even-numbered rows are purl, worked from left to right (except the moss st panel).

CHART 2

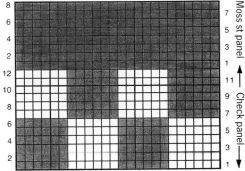

Moss st panel
Check panel

#### Divide for fronts and back

With right side facing join on A and B and patt 54 sts, keeping checks correct, then join on small ball of C and work 10 sts in m st (64 sts), then turn. Keeping a 10 st border of m st in C at armhole edge, work on these sts as follows:
**Next 11 rows** work in A and B in check patt from chart 2.
**Next 8 rows** work in C in m st.
**Next 12 rows** work in A and B in check patt from chart 2.

CHART 3

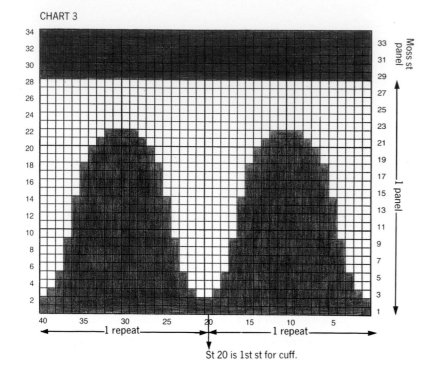

Moss st panel

1 panel

1 repeat — 1 repeat

St 20 is 1st st for cuff.

**Next 8 rows** work in C in m st.
Rep these last 20 rows once, then work 12 rows in A and B in check patt from chart 2 and 2 rows in C in m st.

## Neck shaping
With right side facing bind off 16 sts, m st to end.
**Next row** m st.
**Next row** k2 tog, m st to end.
**Next row** m st.
Rep last 2 rows once, then cut off C (46 sts).
Join on A and B and, keeping a 10 st border of m st at armhole edge, work 12 rows check patt from chart 2 decreasing 1 st at neck edge on first and each alternate row until 40 sts rem. Cut off A and B. Join on C and work 6 rows m st. Slip sts onto a st holder for right front shoulder. Slip next 16 sts onto a st holder for underarm. Join on C and work 10 sts in m st. Join on A and B and work 108 sts in check patt from chart 2, beg with k6 in A. Join on another small ball of C and work 10 more sts in m st (128 sts). Work on these sts for back. Keeping 10 sts at each end of row worked in C in m st, work straight as chart 2 as follows:
**Next 11 rows** work in A and B in check patt from chart 2.
**Next 8 rows** work in C in m st.
**Next 12 rows** work in A and B in check patt from chart 2.
**Next 8 rows** work in C in m st.
Rep these last 20 rows twice, then work 12 rows in A and B in check patt from chart 2 and 2 rows in C in m st.
**Next row** m st 42 sts (right side facing), k2 tog, turn.
**Next row** k2 tog, m st to end.

**Next row** m st to last 2 sts, k2 tog.
**Next row** k2 tog, m st to end (40 sts), then slip sts onto a st holder for right back shoulder.
With right side facing slip next 40 sts onto a st holder for back neck, then work rem 44 sts as follows in C:
**Next row** k2 tog, patt to end.
**Next row** patt to last 2 sts, k2 tog.
Rep these 2 rows once (40 sts), then slip sts onto a st holder for left back shoulder. Slip next 16 sts onto a st holder for underarm, then work rem 64 sts. Join on C and m st 10 sts, then join on A and B and work 54 sts in check patt from chart 2, keeping a 10 st border of m st at armhole edge. Cont as follows:
**Next 11 rows** work in A and B in check patt from chart 2.
**Next 8 rows** work in C in m st.
**Next 12 rows** work in A and B in check patt from chart 2.
**Next 8 rows** work in C in m st.
Rep these last 20 rows once, then work 12 rows in A and B in check patt from chart 2 and 1 row in C in m st.
**Next row** With wrong side facing, bind off 16 sts, m st to end.
**Next row** m st.
**Next row** k2 tog, m st to end.
Rep last 2 rows twice and then cut off C (45 sts).
Join on A and B and, keeping a 10 st border of m st at armhole edge, work 10 rows check patt from chart 2 decreasing 1 st at neck edge on every alternate row until 40 sts rem. Work final 2 rows check patt, then cut off A and B. Join on C and work 6 rows m st. Slip these sts onto a st holder. Weave in any loose ends using a darning needle. Block (see page 155) garment and press carefully on wrong side using a damp cloth.

## Shoulder seams
Graft (see page 155) right front shoulder to right back shoulder (right sides tog). Rep for other shoulder.

## Finishing center back vent
**Left side** With right side facing and size 2 (2¼ mm) needles and 2 strands C, pick up and k 38 sts from bottom of vent to beg of 1st m st band and 25 sts from there to top of ribbed waist (63 sts). Then work 5 rows m st, inc 1 st at shaped edge of vent on every row (68 sts).
**Next row** bind off 56 sts in m st (right side facing), leaving rem 12 sts on a spare needle.
**Right side** With size 2 (2¼ mm) needles and 2 strands C, pick up and k 25 sts from top of ribbed waist to bottom of 1st band of m st and 38 sts from there to end of vent (63 sts). Then work 5 rows m st, inc 1 st at shaped edge of vent on every row (68 sts) and leave sts on needle. Graft (see page 155) 12 sts on spare needle for left side of vent to matching 12 sts on needle for right side of vent (right sides facing). Bind off rem 56 sts of right side of vent. Top stitch increased edges of m st to vent of garment neatly.

## Finishing front edges
**Right edge** With right side facing and size 2 (2¼ mm) needles and 2 strands C, pick up and k 142 sts between bottom edge of peplum and neck edge. Work 6 rows m st, then bind off loosely in m st.
**Left edge** Work as right edge, but pick up sts from neck edge to bottom edge.

## Finishing bottom edges of peplum
With right side facing and size 2 (2¼ mm) needles and 2 strands C, pick up and k 164 sts along bottom edge of right side. Work 6 rows m st, then bind off loosely in m st. Rep for left side. Weave in any loose ends using a darning needle (do not just cut them off), then press carefully on wrong side using a damp cloth.

## COLLAR
**Important** When working collar, its right side will be facing you when wrong side of fronts and back are facing; this is so that when it is folded back on the finished garment, its right side is uppermost.
With right side facing and size 2 (2¼ mm) needles and 2 strands C, beg at inner edge of right front band and pick up and k 32 sts up right front neck edge, rib 40 sts on st holder at back of neck, then pick up and k 32 sts down left front neck edge to inner edge of left front band (104 sts). Cont with 2 strands C.
**Next row** m st 6, work in k1 p1 rib to last 6 sts, m st 6. Rep this row 6 more times.
**Next row** m st 6, p2 tog, *rib 8, p2 tog; rep from * to last 6 sts, m st 6 (94 sts).
**Next row** m st 6 in C, join on b (use single strand, but twist in another ball of B at back to maintain even thickness) and k to last 6 sts. Join on small ball of C, m st 6 in C.

**Next row** m st 6 in C, p to last 6 sts in B, m st 6 in C. Rep these last 2 rows twice.

**Next row** m st 6 in C, in B, k1, *inc into next st, k7; rep from * to last 7 sts, k1, m st 6 in C (104 sts).

**Next 3 rows** work straight in B with m st borders in C at each end.

**Next row** m st 6 in C, in B, k2, *k3, inc into next st; rep from * to last 8 sts, k2, m st 6 in C (126 sts).

Change to size 3 (3¼ mm) needles and work 3 rows straight in B with m st borders in C at each end.

**Next row** m st 6, *k2, inc into next st; rep from * to last 6 sts, m st 6 (164 sts). Then work 3 rows straight in B with m st borders in C at each end, then work from chart 3, beg at st 1, row 1 and keeping patt correct, as follows:

**Row 1** m st 6 in C, in B, *patt 18, inc into next st; rep from * to last 6 sts, m st 6 in C (172 sts).

**Rows 2–6** as chart.

**Row 7** m st 6 in C, in A and B, k1, inc into next st, *patt 16, inc into next st, patt 2, inc into next st; rep from * to last 24 sts, k16, inc into next st, k1, m st 6 in C (188 sts).

**Rows 8–16** as chart, working extra sts in A.

**Row 17** m st 6 in C, in A and B, k4, inc into next st, *patt 12, inc into next st, patt 8, inc into next st; rep from * to last 23 sts, patt 12, inc into next st, patt 4, m st 6 in C (204 sts).

**Rows 18–22** as chart, working extra sts in A. Cut off B. Keeping m st border at each end and with A (twisting in an extra ball of A at back of work to keep thickness even), cont as follows:

**Row 23** m st 6 in C, in A, *patt 7, inc into next st; rep from * to last 6 sts, m st 6 in C (228 sts).

**Rows 24–28** as chart, then cut off A.

**Next 6 rows** with 2 strands C, work in m st. Bind off loosely in m st.

## SLEEVES

With size 3 (3¼ mm) needles and B, cast on 118 sts. Weaving in an extra ball of B at back of work, work 16 rows in St st. Cut off extra strand B.

*Join on A and work rows 1–7 of chart 4, beg at st 1, row 1, then cut off B. Join on C and work rows 8–12 of chart 4, then cut off A. Cont in C and work 30 rows in St st, weaving in a 2nd ball of C at back of work, then cut off 1 strand C. Join on A and work rows 1–7 of chart 4, then cut off C. Join on B and work rows 8–12 of chart 4, then cut off A*. Cont in B and work 30 rows in St st, weaving in a 2nd ball of B, then cut off 1 strand B. Rep from * to * once, then cont in B and work 16 rows in St st, weaving in 3rd ball of B. Do not bind off.

Press carefully on wrong side using a damp cloth. Graft (see page 155) cast-on edge to sts on needle (right sides tog). Weave in loose ends using a darning needle.

## Cuffs

With set of 4 double-pointed size 2 (2¼ mm) needles and 2 strands C, pick up and k 112 sts around bottom edge of sleeve. Join.

**Next round** *k2 tog; rep from * to end (56 sts).

**Next round** *k1, p1, k1, p2 tog; rep from * to last 6 sts, k1, p1, k1, p3 tog (44 sts).

Work 10 more rounds in k1 p1 rib, then cut off both strands of C. Join on B and k 1 round.

**Next round** k, inc into every st (88 sts).

**Next round** k4, *k6, inc into next st; rep from * to end (100 sts).

Join on A and, beg with st 20, row 3 of chart 3, and continuing in rounds, work rounds 3–6.

**Round 7** inc into 1st st, inc into next st, *k18, inc into next st, inc into next st; rep from * to last 18 sts, k18 (110 sts).

**Rounds 8–11** as chart, working extra sts in A.

**Round 12** k4, inc into next st, *k16, inc into next st, k4, inc into next st; rep from * to last 17 sts, k16, inc into next st (120 sts).

**Rounds 13–16** as chart.

**Round 17** k6, inc into next st, *k14, inc into next st, k8, inc into next st; rep from * to last 17 sts, k14, inc into next st, k2 (130 sts).

**Rounds 18–26** as chart, then cut off A and B. Join on C (single strand), and k 1 round, then work 5 rounds m st. Bind off loosely in m st. Rep for 2nd cuff.

## Sleeve insertion

With sleeve folded along underarm seam, make box pleat (see page 157) in panel at top of sleeve so that center of pleat is on foldline of sleeve and aligns with shoulder seam of jacket. With a size 2 (2¼ mm) circular needle and C, pick up and k 130 sts around top edge of sleeve. Place sleeve in armhole of jacket and, with box pleat at shoulder seam and right sides together, graft (see page 155) together, beg with the 16 sts on st holder for armhole. Rep for 2nd sleeve.

## FINISHING

Weave in any rem loose ends using a darning needle, block (see page 155) garment and give a final careful press on wrong side using a damp cloth, but do not press ribbing. Sew on buttons to right front band, then sew 8 snap fasteners to front bands to secure.

CHART 4

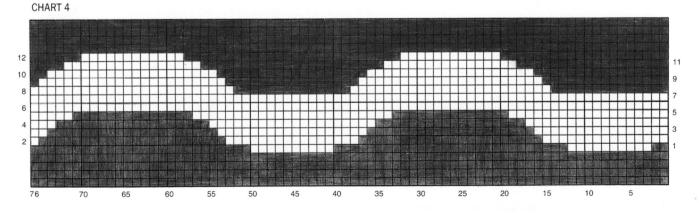

Odd-numbered rows are knit, worked from right to left (except the moss st panel).
Even-numbered rows are purl, worked from left to right (except the moss st panel).

# AUTUMN LEAF SWEATER

From the converted cowshed in which I work I can see an ancient wood. Oaks tower up, and in autumn the entire wood turns a mass of gold and russet – the colors traditionally associated with natural dyes. Used too often they can lose their impact, becoming sludgy and dull, so I have livened up the design by brightening the colors of the leaves. Natural dyes are versatile enough to make us believe that leaves really are these colors, and I enjoyed using walnuts and onion skins to dye the background. The design is knitted on circular needles, starting at the bottom rib and knitting up. This is a simple design to knit and looks gorgeous.

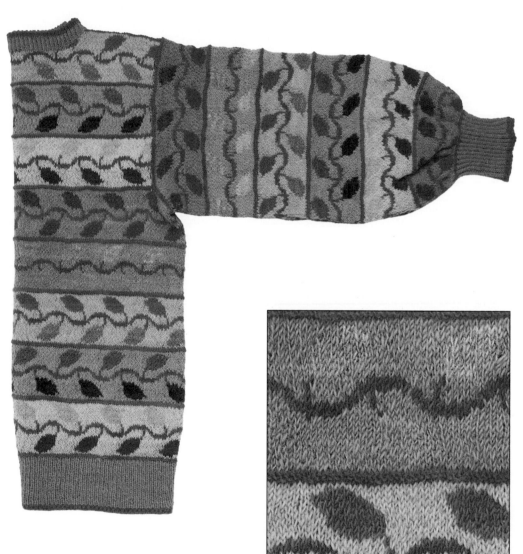

## MATERIALS

Pair of size 2 (2¼ mm) needles
Circular size 2 (2¼ mm) needle 16 in (40 cm) long
Set of 4 double-pointed size 2 (2¼ mm) needles
Pair of size 3 (3¼ mm) needles
Circular size 3 (3¼ mm) needle 29 in (73.5 cm) long
Set of 4 double-pointed size 3 (3¼ mm) needles
7 stitch holders

## WEIGHT OF YARN AND COLORS

Walnut (A)    10 oz (280 g)
Pale walnut (B)    8 oz (230 g)
Ochre (C)    6 oz (170 g)
Elderberry (D)    1 oz (28 g)
Buttercup yellow (E)    2 oz (57 g)
Navy (F)    2 oz (57 g)
Grass green (G)    2 oz (57 g)
Blue-green (H)    1 oz (28 g)
Redwood pink (I)    2 oz (57 g)

## MEASUREMENTS

Length from top of shoulder to bottom edge of sweater:
28 in (71 cm)
Actual width all around at underarm: 42 in (106 cm)
Sleeve length: 22½ in (57 cm)

## GAUGE

Over pattern, using size 3 (3¼ mm) needles (or size to obtain guage), 33 sts and 32 rows to 4 in (10 cm).

## IMPORTANT

● Twist wools at back of work every 1–2 sts to avoid making holes, but do not pull tight.
● When working St st using just one color, twist a spare ball of the same color yarn across the back of work to keep the thickness of the garment even.
● To make ridge on right side of work between each panel, round 2 of the chart is purl when using the circular needle and rows 1 and 2 are knit when 2 needles are being used.
● The sweater is knitted on a circular needle as far as the underarm, so every round of the chart up to that point is knit (except round 2, which is purl).
● When working in rounds for the sleeves, remember to work chart in reverse order as you are knitting from shoulder to cuff, that is, you work from round 26 to 1. Round 1 of the chart is purl.
● When using the circular needle, loop a short strand of brightly colored wool around the first stitch each time you begin a round so that you can find the beginning easily.
● Before beginning each new panel, check with the diagram (above right) to ensure that you have the correct color combination.

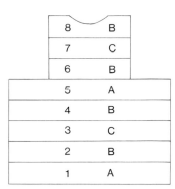

## Key

**A** = background B, leaf 1 D, leaf 2 E
**B** = background A, leaf 1 F, leaf 2 G
**C** = background B, leaf 1 H, leaf 2 I
(The sweater in the photographs has been knitted using additional colours in an alternative combination.)
The edges of the ribbing, the stems of the leaves and rounds 1 and 2 of all panels are worked in C.
Work the 6 panels of sleeve with the color combinations in the following order: panel 1 in B, panel 2 in C, panel 3 in B, panel 4 in A, panel 5 in B, and panel 6 in C.

## INSTRUCTIONS

### FRONT AND BACK

With size 2 (2¼ mm) circular needle and 2 strands C, cast on 264 sts and work 2 rounds in k1 p1 rib. Join on 2 strands A and work 27 rounds in k1 p1 rib. Cont with single strand.

**Inc round** *k2, inc into next st; rep from * to end (352 sts).

Change to size 3 (3¼ mm) circular needle and work from chart, beg at row 2, st 1 (p in C). Work straight until 5 complete panels, with color combinations in order A, B, C, B and A, have been worked.

### Divide for front and back

Slip 1st 16 sts onto a st holder (holder 1), then with pair of size 3 (3¼ mm) needles and C, patt 144 sts, turn. Leave rem sts on circular needle. Work straight until panels 6 and 7, using color combinations B and C, have been worked. Then work rows 1–18 of panel 8 in color combination B.

**Row 19** patt 44 sts. K2 tog, turn.

**Rows 20–26** dec 1 st at neck edge every row (38 sts).
**Rows 1 and 2** as chart, then slip sts onto a st holder for shoulder. Slip next 52 sts onto a st holder for neck, then cont on rem 46 sts as follows:

**Row 19** With right side facing, k2 tog, patt to end.
**Rows 20–26** dec 1 st at neck edge every row (38 sts).
**Rows 1 and 2** as chart, then slip sts onto a st holder. With right side facing, return to rem 192 sts and slip next 32 sts onto a st holder (holder 2). With pair of size 3 (3¼ mm) needles and color combination B, patt 144 sts and slip rem 16 sts onto holder 1. Work straight until panels 6 and 7, using color combinations B and C, have

been worked. Then work rows 1–18 of panel 8 in color combination B.

**Row 19** patt 44 sts, k2 tog, turn.

**Rows 20–26** dec 1 st at neck edge every row (38 sts), then slip sts onto a st holder. Slip next 52 sts onto a st holder, then cont on rem 46 sts as follows:

**Row 19** k2 tog, patt to end.
**Rows 20–26** dec 1 st at neck edge every row (38 sts). Leave sts on needle.

### Shoulder seams

Block (see page 155) garment and press carefully on wrong side using a damp cloth. Graft (see page 155) right front shoulder to right back shoulder (right sides together). Rep for left shoulder. Weave in any loose ends using a darning needle (do not just cut them off).

### SLEEVES

**Remember** to k all rounds (except round 1, which is p) and work panels in rev order – from round 26–1.
With size 3 (3¼ mm) circular needle and right side facing and C, slip last 16 sts from holder 1 onto left needle and k them. Pick up and k 144 sts around armhole and then k the rem 16 sts from holder (176 sts).

K 1 round and p 1 round in C, then work from chart, beg at st 1, round 26 of bottom panel of chart, until 6 panels have been worked, ending with round 5.

**Round 4** k2, *k1, k2 tog; rep from * to end (118 sts). Change to set of 4 double-pointed size 2 (2¼ mm) needles.

**Round 3** k2, *k2 tog; rep from * to end (60 sts).

**Rounds 2 and 1** k 1 round and p 1 round in C. Join on 2 strands A and work 25 rounds in k1 p1 rib. Then join on 2 strands C, work 2 rounds in k1 p1 rib and bind off loosely in rib. Rep for 2nd sleeve. Weave in any loose ends using a darning needle and press carefully on wrong side using a damp cloth.

### NECKBAND

With right side facing and set of 4 double-pointed size 2 (2¼ mm) needles and A, k the 52 sts for back of neck, pick up and k 20 sts down left side of neck, k the 52 sts for front of neck and then pick up and k 20 sts up right side of neck (144 sts). Work 8 rounds in k1 p1 rib. Join on C, work 2 rounds in k1 p1 rib, p 1 round work 2 more rounds in k1 p1 rib, then join on A. Work 7 more rounds in k1 p1 rib then bind off loosely in rib. Fold band to inside along foldline and stitch down neatly.

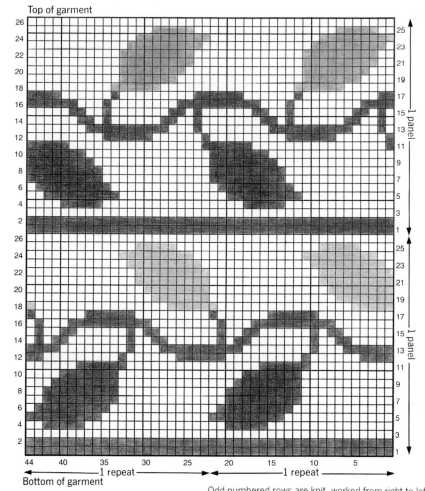

Top of garment

Bottom of garment

1 repeat    1 repeat

1 panel

1 panel

Odd-numbered rows are knit, worked from right to left.
Even-numbered rows are purl, worked from left to right.

# IONIC COLUMNS JACKET

I'd been wanting to design something architectural for years before finally perfecting this pattern. If nothing else, it's taught me the difference between Doric, Corinthian and Ionic columns. The ribs are Roman bricks. This is one of my favorite recent designs, simply because it is so striking – the pattern doesn't repeat, and neither the front, back nor sleeves match. Because it's so original and sophisticated, it's great fun to wear.

## WEIGHT OF YARN AND COLORS
Medium indigo blue (A)   10 oz (280 g)
Gray (B)   8 oz (230 g)
Navy (C)   8 oz (230 g)
Pale walnut (D)   6 oz (170 g)
Burgundy (E1)   2 oz (57 g)
Madder (E2)   2 oz (57 g)
Redwood pink (E3)   2 oz (57 g)

## MEASUREMENTS
Length from top of shoulder to bottom edge of jacket: 23 in (58 cm)
Actual width all around at underarm: 51 in (129.5 cm)
Sleeve length: 18 in (46 cm)

## GAUGE
Over pattern, using size 3 (3¼ mm) needles (or size to obtain gauge), 30 stitches and 30 rows to 4 in (10 cm).

## IMPORTANT
- Twist wools at back of work every 1–2 sts to avoid making holes, but do not pull tight.
- This garment is knitted sideways, beginning at right front edge.
- When working the brick pattern, change color of bricks every 2–3 rows to add texture.
- When working St st using just one color twist a spare ball of the same color yarn across the back of work to keep the thickness of the garment even.
- The number of rows on the shoulders and underarms varies. This is in the design of the garment so do not be concerned.

## MATERIALS
Pair of size 2 (2¼ mm) needles
Set of 4 double-pointed size 2 (2¼ mm) needles
Pair of size 3 (3¼ mm) needles
Circular size 3 (3¼ mm) needle 16 in (40 cm) long
1 stitch holder
7 buttons

## INSTRUCTIONS
### FRONTS AND BACK
With size 3 (3¼ mm) needles and A, cast on 140 sts and, beg with k row, work 2 rows in St st. Then work from chart 1, beg at st 1, row 1.
Rows 1–6 as chart.
Rows 7 and 9 inc 1 st at beg of row (neck edge), then cont as chart but work each alternate row as follows:
Rows 11 and 13 cast on 2 sts at beg of row (neck edge).
Rows 15 and 17 cast on 3 sts at beg of row (neck edge).
Rows 19 and 21 cast on 5 sts at beg of row (neck edge; 162 sts).
Rows 22–68 as chart.
Row 69 bind off 60 sts (102 sts).
Rows 70–84 as chart.
Rows 85–95 as chart, beg row 87 with k4 in B (these rows will be referred to later as one block of bricks).
Rows 96–100 work in A.
Rows 101–112 work in A from chart 2.
Rows 113–116 as chart.
Row 117 cast on 60 sts (162 sts).
Rows 118–168 as chart.
Row 169 bind off 2 sts at beg of row (neck edge).
Row 170 as chart.
Row 171 k2 tog (neck edge), patt to end.
Rows 172–173 as chart.
Row 174 work as chart to last 2 sts, p2 tog (neck edge; 158 sts).
Rows 175–200 as chart.
Rows 201–205 work from chart 3.
Row 206 work as chart to last st, inc into last st (neck edge).
Rows 207–209 as chart.
Row 210 work as chart to last st, inc into last st (neck edge).
Rows 211 and 212 as chart.
Row 213 cast on 2 sts at beg of row (neck edge; 162 sts).
Rows 214–264 as chart.
Row 265 bind off 60 sts at beg of row (102 sts).
Rows 266–300 as chart.
Rows 301–314 work from chart 4.
Row 315 cast on 60 sts at beg of row (162 sts).
Rows 316–368 as chart.
Rows 369–371 bind off 5 sts at beg of this and next alternate row (neck edge).
Row 372 as chart.
Rows 373 and 375 bind off 3 sts at beg of row (neck edge).
Row 376 as chart.
Rows 377 and 379 bind off 2 sts at beg of this and next alternate row (neck edge).
Row 380 as chart.
Rows 381 and 383 bind off 1 st at beg of this and next alternate row (neck edge).
Rows 384–388 as chart, then bind off loosely. Weave in any loose ends using a darning needle (do not just cut them off). Block (see page 155) garment and press carefully on wrong side using a damp cloth.

### Shoulder seams
With right side facing and size 3 (3¼ mm) needles and B, pick up and k 51 sts along back right shoulder, then slip sts onto a st holder.
With right side facing and size 3 (3¼ mm) needles and B, pick up and k 51 sts along front right shoulder. Next row p.
Work 1 complete block of bricks (see rows 87–95, chart 1), beg row 1 with k2 in B and end with 2 rows in B. Then graft (see page 155) right front shoulder to right back shoulder (right sides together). Rep for left shoulder.

### SLEEVES
#### Right sleeve
With size 3 (3¼ mm) needles and A, cast on 115 sts. Work from chart 5, beg at st 1, row 1 and work rows 1–164. Keep sts on needle and graft (see page 155) them to cast-on edge (right sides together).

#### Left sleeve
Work as right sleeve, but work from chart 5 beg at st 1 row 81.
Work rows 81–164 as chart, then work rows 1–80 as chart. Keep sts on needle and graft as for right sleeve.

#### Cuffs
With right side facing and set of 4 double-pointed size 2 (2¼ mm) needles and A, pick up and k 132 sts (44 sts per needle) around bottom edge of sleeve.
Round 1 *k4, k2 tog; rep from * to end (110 sts).
Round 2 *k3, k2 tog; rep from * to end (88 sts).
Round 3 *k8, k2 tog; rep from * to last 8 sts, k8 (80 sts).
Rounds 4–32 join on B and work 3 complete blocks of bricks (see rows 85–93, chart 1, but remember to k every round), beg and end with 2 rows in B and working 2 rounds in B between blocks of bricks and 1 st in B between each brick.
Round 33 p (to make foldline).
Work 30 more rounds in k1 p1 rib in B, then bind off loosely in rib. Fold cuff to inside along foldline and stitch down neatly.

### WELT
With right side facing and size 2 (2¼ mm) needles and B, pick up and k 371 sts along bottom edge of fronts and back. P1 row.
Rows 1–29 work 3 complete blocks of bricks (see rows 85–93, chart 1), beg and end with 2 rows in B, and beg and end each row with 2 sts in B.
Row 30 k (to make foldline).
Work 30 more rows in B in k1 p1 rib, then bind off loosely in rib.
Fold welt to inside along foldline and stitch down neatly.

### NECKBAND
With right side facing and size 2 (2¼ mm) needles and B, pick up and k 131 sts around neck. P 1 row.
Rows 1–20 work 2 complete blocks of bricks (see rows 85–93, chart 1), beg and end with 2 rows in B and beg and end each row with 2 sts in B.
Row 21 p (to make foldline).
Work 2 more complete blocks of bricks (20 rows), beg and end with 2 rows in B, then bind off loosely. Fold band to inside along foldline and stitch down neatly.

### BUTTONHOLE BAND
With size 2 (2¼ mm) needles and B, pick up and k 211 sts from bottom edge of welt up to beg of neckband (do not include side edge of neckband itself).
Rows 1–9 beg with a p row. Work 1 block of bricks (see rows 85–93, chart 1), beg and end each row with 1 st in B. Then make buttonholes:
Row 10 in B, k6, *bind off 7, k25 (including st already on needle); rep from * to last 13 sts, bind off 7, k6 (buttonholes will fall in center of alternate bricks).
Row 11 p, casting on 7 sts over the 7 buttonholes.
Rows 12–20 work 1 more complete block of bricks (see rows 87–95, chart 1).
Rows 21 k (to make foldline).
Rows 22–30 work in B in k1 p1 rib.
Rows 31 and 32 as rows 10 and 11, but working in k1 p1 rib.
Rows 33–41 work in k1 p1 rib, then bind off loosely in rib.
Fold band to inside along foldline and stitch down neatly.
Neaten around buttonholes using a small buttonhole st.

### BUTTON BAND
With right side facing and size 2 (2¼ mm) needles and B, pick up and k 211 sts from bottom of neckband (do not include side edge of neckband itself) to bottom edge of welt (right side facing).
Rows 1–20 work 2 complete blocks of bricks (see rows 85–95, chart 1), beg and end each row with 1 st in B.
Row 21 k (to make foldline).
Rows 22–41 work in B in k1 p1 rib, then bind off loosely in rib. Fold band to inside along foldline and stitch down neatly. Sew on buttons.

### ARMHOLE BANDS
With right side facing and size 3 (3¼ mm) circular needle and B, pick up and k 176 sts around top of sleeve.
Rounds 1–11 work 1 complete block of bricks (see rows 85–95, chart 1), beg and end with 2 rows in B, working 1 st in B between each brick. Leave sts on needle.
Important Make sure that the right sleeve is put in the right armhole and the left sleeve in the left armhole. Position sleeve inside armhole (right sides together) and graft (see page 155) tog. Rep for second sleeve.

CHART 1

Cast on edge of right front

Odd-numbered rows are knit, worked from right to left.
Even-numbered rows are purl, worked from left to right.

Armhole

Armhole

CHART 2

Right back

Armhole

Armhole

Back of neck

CHART 3

Left back

Armhole

Armhole

Back of neck

CHART 4

**151**

Left front

Armhole

Armhole

Bind off edge

CHART 5

Bind off edge

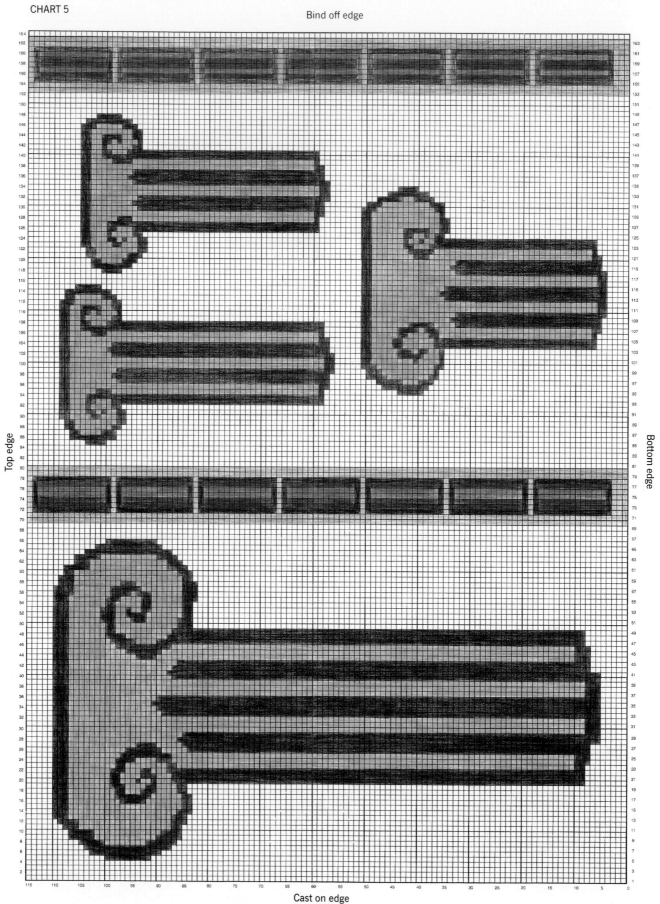

Top edge

Bottom edge

Cast on edge

# GLOSSARY OF KNITTING TERMS AND TECHNIQUES

As an avid knitter myself, I know how exciting it is to have a new pattern and a bag of pure wool: all those wonderful colors! It is a very great temptation to begin knitting without paying heed to the preliminary instructions and helpful hints. All too often, though, this results in disappointment, even disaster. To help you avoid such disappointment, listed below are a number of hints and methods that, if used, will result in a sweater you can be proud of.

## NEEDLES

In the United States knitting needles are sized by number – the higher the number, the larger the needle. Now, metric sizing is being used as well and the smaller the metric size, the smaller the needle. In this book American sizes are given with metric sizes in brackets.

**Knitting needle sizes used in the book**

| U.S. | Metric |
|------|--------|
| 2 | 2¼ mm |
| 3 | 3¼ mm |
| 5 | 4 mm |
| 7 | 4½ mm |
| 8 | 5 mm |

## USING CIRCULAR NEEDLES

These are available in a variety of lengths so, when buying a circular needle for a pattern in the book, look under "Materials" to see which length of needle you need.

Sweaters worked in the round are attractive because there are no seams, which results in a smoother line and, consequently, a better fit. Here are some tips for using a circular needle successfully.
• When working the first round after casting on, make sure the stitches are not twisted around the needle before you knit the first stitch.
• All rounds are knit (unless otherwise stated).
• Loop a short strand of brightly colored wool around the first stitch of each round so that you can find the beginning easily.
• You can knit from circular needles, in rows, instead of using conventional needles when you have a great number of stitches.
• When working in **rows** with a circular needle, when you have worked a row, simply turn the work around and use the right-hand tip of the needle to work along the row in the opposite direction.

## USING A SET OF 4 DOUBLE-POINTED NEEDLES

When you are using a set of 4 double-pointed needles for working cuffs, for example, divide the number to be cast on evenly between 3 of the needles. Using the fourth needle, work all the stitches on the first needle so that they are then on the fourth needle. The first needle is now free. Use this needle to work all the stitches on the second needle and then use this needle to complete the round, working all the stitches on the fourth needle. Work each successive round in this way.

## CASTING ON

There are several ways of casting on, but the one used throughout the book, which produces a very neat edge, is known as the cable method. You need 2 needles, then:
• make a slip knot and place it on the left-hand needle
• insert the right-hand needle through the slip knot and knit it and slip new stitch onto left-hand needle
• insert the right-hand needle between the 2 stitches on the left-hand needle, wind the wool around the tip of the right-hand needle, draw the loop you've made through between the stitches and then slip it onto the left-hand needle
• Repeat this last step until you have cast on the required number of stitches.

## BINDING OFF

Make sure you always bind off in pattern, that is, bind off knit stitches knitwise and purl stitches purlwise unless otherwise stated.

## BINDING OFF KNITWISE

• Knit the first 2 stitches.
• With the left-hand needle, lift the first stitch over the second stitch and drop it off the needle.
• Knit the next stitch and repeat the second step and so on until you have bound off the required number of stitches.

## BINDING OFF PURLWISE

• Purl the first 2 stitches.
• With the left-hand needle, lift the first stitch over the second stitch and drop it off the needle.
• Purl the next stitch and repeat the second step and so on until you have bound off the required number of stiches.

## GAUGE

This is *the* most important thing to get right if the finished sweater is to be a success – if the gauge is not correct, the result can be disastrous. This is because the gauge determines the shape and size of the sweater so any variation, no matter how small, will alter the look of the finished garment. It is, therefore, important that the gauge given at the beginning of each pattern is matched before you start to knit. The size of needle given for each pattern is my own choice, but you may need to use a different size of needle to achieve the correct result.

To find out if you need to use a different size of needle, work a test square. This may seem to be a nuisance and a waste of time, but it will save you the aggravation of a finished sweater that is the wrong size and shape.

Knit the square in pattern or stockinette stitch as directed, casting on about 10 more stitches and working about 10 more rows than the number of stitches or rows to 4 in (10 cm). Lay the finished square on a flat surface and, using a metal tape measure or plastic ruler, count the number of stitches to 4 in (10 cm) one way and the number of rows to 4 in (10 cm) the other, measuring over the center of the square.
• If there are too *many* stitches to 4 in (10 cm), work another test square with *larger* needles.
• If there are too *few* stitches to 4 in (10 cm) try again with *smaller* needles. (It is the gauge that is important, not the needle size.)

Once you have achieved the correct gauge you can rest safe in the knowledge that your finished sweater will work out exactly like the pattern.

## USING CHARTS

Every pattern in this book uses a chart. On the chart, each square represents a stitch and each line of squares represents a row of knitting.

When working from a chart using 2 needles, the knit rows are worked from right to left and the purl rows from left to right. The colors given on the chart correspond to the sweaters in the photographs, but you can, of course, use any colors you like instead. If you do use different colors, it will be easiest if you copy the chart onto graph paper substituting your own colors, but take care to copy it *exactly*, stitch for stitch.

When working from a chart, start at stitch 1, row 1, unless the instructions specify otherwise.

## FAIR ISLE KNITTING

When you are using 2 or more different colors of wool at any one time, carry the yarns not in use across the back of the work, twisting them with the wool in use before you knit the next stitch every 1 to 2 stitches, remembering to stretch the stitches to their correct width to keep them elastic and never pull the floating strands too tight. This will keep your knitting tidy and avoid forming holes.

## INCREASING

### TO INCREASE IN A KNIT STITCH
- Knit into the front of the stitch but do not slip it off the needle.
- Knit into the back of the same stitch, dropping it off the needle.

### TO INCREASE IN A PURL STITCH
- Work as given for knit stitches above but work purlwise.

## DECREASING

### TO DECREASE KNITWISE
- Pass the tip of the right-hand needle into the second stitch on the left-hand needle, then into the first stitch.
- Knit these 2 stitches together, making 1 stitch.

### TO DECREASE PURLWISE
- Pass the tip of the right-hand needle into the front of the first and second stitches on the left-hand needle.
- Purl the 2 stitches together.

### TO DECREASE MORE THAN 1 STITCH
Bind off the required number of stitches using the binding off method given under **Binding off**.

## PICKING UP STITCHES
It is not difficult to achieve a really professional finish when picking up stitches for buttonhole bands or around neck edges as long as you remember the following:
- measure the edge you are picking up stitches along and mark each inch with a pin, divide the number of stitches to be picked up by the measurement and then pick up that number of stitches between each pair of pins.
- never work too close to the edge: put the tip of the

needle through the work 2 strands down (right side facing) from the edge (if you work too near the edge, the result will be uneven).

## HOW TO PICK UP A STITCH
- Insert the tip of the right-hand needle through the work from the right side, wind the wool around the needle and then draw a loop through to the right side – as if you were knitting a stitch.
- Transfer the loop to the left-hand needle and knit it. (Work into small stitches rather than loose loops wherever possible.)

## BLOCKING
This is another important factor in the making of a well-finished sweater. Blocking each piece of knitting once it has been worked is much easier and gives a far better finish than blocking the finished sweater. This is how it is done.
- Turn work to wrong side and pin it to an ironing board, easing it into shape and the required measurements.
- Cover it with a damp cloth and press it lightly with a hot iron, making sure that you do not move the iron to and fro, but press, lift it up, and then press again evenly over the work, omitting any ribbing. (You will fit a sleeve onto your ironing board most of the time, but when you are blocking the front and back of a sweater, pin the shoulder at the top of the board and then smooth it down the length of the board until it is the required length minus the welt, press, then repeat for the next ironing-board width of work and so on. Alternatively, lay a doubled blanket or two large towels on the floor or a large table, pin the front and back of the sweater out to the required measurements and then press.)

It is also very important to keep the work as neat as possible at the back, so weave in all loose ends using a darning needle – never just cut off the loose ends and leave them as even tight knots come undone and the knitting unravels.

## POCKET LININGS
Pockets *can* make a sweater look beautifully finished, but if attention is not paid to the detail of them, they can equally completely spoil it so, when you sew in a pocket lining, remember the following:

- never sew in a pocket lining until the sweater has been blocked and pressed
- pin all the edges of the lining that are to be stitched in place and tack the opening down
- slip stitch the pocket in place by lifting a loop from the edge of the lining and a loop from the back of the main body of work (not a strand that has been carried along at the back) and lift next loop above it for next slip stitch as stitches sewn out of line will prevent the sweater hanging perfectly.

## GRAFTING
This is a means of joining 2 knitted edges together without the bulk that results from binding off and then sewing the edges together. It gives a very smooth appearance so shoulder seams, particularly, look better grafted. Grafting is usually worked before the knitting is removed from the needles, but you will also find in the patterns that you are asked to graft a seam between 2 stitch holders or a needle and a stitch holder or a needle and a cast-on edge.

There are 3 methods of grafting, as follows:

### METHOD 1
- Take the 2 pieces of knitting to be joined together, with the stitches still on the needles, placing the needles parallel to each other with right sides of both pieces together.
- Take a third needle in your right hand, pass its tip through the first stitch on both needles and knit them together as one stitch.
- Repeat the second step for the second stitch and then lift the first stitch over the second stitch and off the right-hand needle just like when you bind off. Continue in this way until all the stitches have been bound off.

### METHOD 2
- Thread a darning needle with a length of the same color wool as the edges you want to join together.
- Abut the edges of the 2 pieces of knitting to be joined together on a flat surface (right sides up).
- Pass the darning needle knitwise through the first stitch on the front needle and slip the stitch off the knitting needle.
- Pass the darning needle purlwise through the second stitch on the same needle, leaving the stitch on the needle.

● Pass the darning needle purlwise through the first stitch on the back needle and slip the stitch off the knitting needle.

● Pass the darning needle knitwise through the second stitch on the back needle, leaving the stitch on the knitting needle.

● Rep this process, from the third step above, until all the stitches have been joined together, then pull the strand of wool so as to form stitches of the same size as the knitted ones (holding the other end at the beginning of the row) and finish off by darning in the loose ends at the back of the piece of knitting.

## METHOD 3
### Joining sleeve seams

● Slip the stitches left on the needle onto a double-pointed needle.

● With right sides together, place the stitches on the double-pointed needle against the cast-on edge.

● Using one of a pair of needles, insert the tip through the 1st stitch on the double-pointed needle and then through the 1st stitch of the row of knitting below the cast-on edge.

● Wind the wool around the needle and draw a loop through both stitches, as if knitting a stitch.

● Repeat with the 2nd stitch on the double-pointed needle and the 2nd stitch on the cast-on edge, so that there are 2 stitches on the right-hand needle.

● Using the double-pointed needle, lift the 1st stitch over the 2nd stitch and drop it off (as in binding off).

● Repeat until the end of the row has been reached and all the stitches bound off.

### Inserting a sleeve

● Slip the stitches left on the needle onto a circular needle.

● With the right sides together, insert the sleeve into the armhole and work as for joining sleeve seams (above).

## RIBBING

The ribbing for the button bands, cuffs, welts, and so on of some of the garments in the book are of double thickness. This gives a smarter finish and results in a more professional look. When the ribbing is double thickness, a ridge is worked halfway through. This is referred to in all the patterns as the foldline and this

foldline must always be on the outside of the finished garment. The ribbing is then stitched neatly into place on the wrong side.

## BUTTONHOLES

Good buttonholes are an important part of the finished sweater and so it is well worth giving them some close attention. Instructions for making the buttonholes are given in each pattern, but it is essential to reinforce them when the garment is finished otherwise they will not hold together, be easy to use, or provide a professional finish.

One of the best ways to reinforce buttonholes is the following method. On either vertical or horizontal buttonholes, work neat buttonhole stitches along each side. The stitches should be almost touching and of an even size, but they should not be squashed too closely together as this will stretch the buttonhole out of shape. At either end of the buttonhole, as you come to them, work 3 straight stitches.

## PLEATS

The sleeves of some of the garments have pleats and these are made before the sleeves are put into the armholes. Be sure to make the folds as instructed. Pin them first so that you can check that they are each of equal size and evenly spaced and only then stitch them in place, stitching through all 3 thicknesses of the pleat.

## FRILLS

At first sight the frills look a daunting prospect, but if you follow the instructions step by step, they are not difficult at all and will give you a great sense of pride and satisfaction when you have finished the sweater. Bear the following in mind:
● make sure that the frills are turned down onto the right side of the work before you start a new frill
● pick up the stitches for each new frill along the rows indicated by the markers
● when you are working frills along the neck edge and at the wrists, pick up the stitches on the inside of the work.

## DORSET CROSSWHEEL BUTTONS

These handmade buttons have been used on all the cardigans in the book and add a special touch to the finished sweater. Use the main color for the edge and highlight colors to work the center – you will be surprised how easy these buttons are to make.

### MATERIALS

Plastic or brass curtain rings to fit buttonholes
Darning needle
Strands of yarn in 3 colors (A, B, C)

### INSTRUCTIONS

Hold the ring and tie the strand of A to it. Thread the darning needle with the other end and work buttonhole stitch all round the ring, joining the wool to the first stitch and completely covering the ring with the knot of the stitches on the inside. Join the strand of B to the ring and work 8 spokes by winding the strand around the ring so that each spoke consists of a front and a back strand, twisting in the center, keeping the spokes equal distances apart. Wind firmly but not too tightly and finish by working a firm cross stitch in the center that holds all the strands together. Weave in the loose ends. Join on the strand of C at the back of the center of the button and bring it through to the front. Backstitch in a clockwise fashion, back over one spoke, then pass the needle under the next spoke, backstitch over that and so on to produce a spider's web pattern. Leave a tiny gap between the edge of the backstitching and the buttonhole edge and weave in the ends.

## CROCHET

### CHAIN STITCH

● Make a slip knot and insert the hook.
● With the wool looped over your index finger, push the hook through the first knot and catch it on the yarn. Pull the yarn through the first knot to form a new loop on hook.
● Repeat until you have the required number of chains.

### SINGLE CROCHET

● Insert the hook into the 2nd chain from the hook, with the yarn around the hook draw through a loop, place the yarn around the hook, draw through 2 loops.

### HALF DOUBLE CROCHET

● Yarn around the hook, then insert the hook into the 3rd chain from the hook, with the yarn around the hook draw a loop, place the yarn around the hook, draw through 3 loops.

### DOUBLE CROCHET

● Yarn around the hook, then insert the hook into the 4th chain from the hook, with the yarn around the hook draw through a loop, place the yarn around the hook and draw through 2 loops, place the yarn around the hook and draw through last 2 loops.

### CHAIN STITCH (EMBROIDERY)

● Bring the needle out on the centerline. Insert the needle back in the same point and, with the thread *under* the tip of the needle, bring the needle out again at a point slightly below. Continue to make stitches by inserting the needle at the point where the thread emerges.

# SUPPLIERS

There are bound to be some people who don't have the time or space to attempt natural dyeing, but who would love to knit these patterns using naturally dyed yarns. Complete kits for all the patterns are available, as are 4 oz (115 g) balls of the individual colors for those who have difficulty with dyeing a particular shade. For either a kit or yarn please send an SAE for the current price list to:

The Natural Dye Company
Stanbridge
Wimborne
Dorset BH21 4JD, England
Tel: (0258) 840549

The wool used in the book is 9 count singles Cheviot scoured (knits as a 4 ply).
Rowan Yarns produce a similar yarn, which is an undyed natural scoured light tweed (ref. no. 201). This yarn can be obtained from many good quality knitting stores, but in case of difficulty please write to the address below for suppliers:

Westminster Trading Company
5 Northern Boulevard
Amherst, NH 03031
Tel: 603 886 5041

Rowan Yarns also do a good selection of yarns and colors in 4 ply wool. These are readily available from most good wool stores, but are not naturally dyed.

Yarns suitable for dyeing, dyestuffs, and dyeing equipment can be obtained from:

Yarn Barn
Box 334
918 Massachusetts Street
Lawrence, KS 66044
Tel: 913 842 4333
Tel: 800 468 0035

The Fiber Studio
P.O. Box 637
Foster Hill Road
Henniker, NH 03242
Tel: 603 428 7830

The Wool Works
1812 North Farwell Avenue
Milwaukee, WI 53202
Tel: 414 278 8838

Custom Handweavers
75 Arbor Road
Menlo Park, CA 94025
Tel: 415 325 0626

Beck's Warp'N Weave & Needlecrafts
2815 34th Street
Lubbock, TX 97410
Tel: 806 799 0151

Serendipity Shop
2 Prairie Street
Park Ridge, IL 60068
Tel: 708 692 7177

Straw Into Gold
3006 San Pablo Avenue
Berkeley, CA 94702
Tel: 415 548 5241
(Yarn only)

JaggerSpun
Water Street
Springvale, ME 04083
Tel: 207 324 4455
(Yarn only)

The Naked Lamb
Route 1, Box 511
Eastsound, WA 98245
Tel: 206 376 4606

Yarnworks
519 Main Street
Grand Junction, CO 81501
Tel: 303 243 5365

The Weavers Store
11 South 9th Street
Columbia, MO 65201
Tel: 314 442 5413

# ACKNOWLEDGMENTS

**A Passion for Color** is the outcome of fourteen years of experimentation and hard work, and it would be impossible to name all the knitters, friends and customers who have so generously helped and encouraged me. My long-suffering team of knitters has taught me the virtue of simplicity, friends have praised and prodded at exactly the right moment, whilst my early customers provided what every fledgeling business most needs – the confidence to expand and take risks. Other debts must also be acknowledged: David for his patience, our children Gracie and Thomas for inspiring the first jerseys, my sister Judy Snape for introducing me to natural dyes, Tony Williams for his invaluable help with the dyeing recipes, and Astrid Garran for being such an enthusiastic and supportive assistant. Cortina Butler, my editor, has been an oasis of calm amidst the chaos. I couldn't have managed without Debbie Packer and Moyra Hilton, who have spent more hours than I care to count working on the patterns.

Then there are my knitters. They are a wonderful team, many have become friends, and I am certainly a lot wiser for the years we've spent together. So a big thank you to Renee Bryant, Mrs Cooper, Mrs Entecott, Mrs Eltringham, Mrs Gillingham, Mrs Green, Chris Harvey, Mrs Kunze, Cary Murrow, Muriel Marchment, Diane Payne, Mrs Davis, Mrs Pope, Mary Reedy, Mrs Whiting, Mrs Newman, Mrs Walmely, Mrs Harris, Mrs Eaton, Mrs Dredge, Mrs Legg, Mrs White, June Feeley, Ann Harris, Barbara Hooker, Mrs Jenkinson, Pat Rawles, Madge Stubbings, Jan Wright, Margaret Ashby, Janice Burke, Ann Carter, Lindsay Chant, Kathy Chappell, Ann Cave, Grace Davies, Mrs Densley, Linda Bennett, Jenny Wood, Shirley Cronin, just to mention a few of my wonderful knitters. Thank you also to Debbie Packer and Pam Price for helping me look after them.

It is curious to spend fourteen years developing something which overnight has become ecologically fashionable. Fashion is a fickle mistress, but here I hope the glories of natural color will help prove it more than a whim. To all those who shared my beliefs and wrote about me when a less concerned view prevailed, one final thank you.

# PICTURE CREDITS

The publisher thanks the following photographers and organizations for their kind permission to reproduce the photographs in this book:
8 David Burnett; 10–11 Simon McBride; 25 above centre Andrew Lawson; 25 below centre George Wright; 27 above centre George Wright; 27 below centre George Wright; 29 above centre Pictures Colour Library; 29 below centre Simon McBride; 33 above centre Landscape Only; 33 below centre Landscape Only; 38 right Tim Woodcock; 44 right Simon McBride; 50 right Zefa Picture Library; 59 George Wright; 62 right Andrew Lawson; 68 right Landscape Only; 74 right John Heseltine; 84 right Mike Buselle's Photo Library; 89 Photos Horticultural; 90 right Zefa Picture Library; 106 right Eric Crichton; 113 Linda Burgess/Insight Picture Library; 118 right George Wright; 136 right S & O Mathews; 141 Landscape Only; 127 Pictures Colour Library; 132 Robert Estall; 146 below left Linda Burgess/Insight Picture Library; 146 below right Andrew Lawson.

The following photographs were taken especially for Conran Octopus:

**Jan Baldwin** 14–23, 25 above, 25 below, 27 above, 27 below, 29 above, 29 below, 30–31, 33 above, 33 below, 34–35, 153, 156.

**Paul Chave** 12–13, 38 left, 39–40, 44 left, 50 left, 52, 56, 62 left, 63, 68 left, 74 left, 75, 78, 84 left, 87, 90 left, 96, 98, 102, 106 left, 112, 115, 118 left, 124, 130, 136 left, 142, 146 above.

**Anthony Crickmay** 1–7, 35 (inset), 37, 42–43, 47, 48–49, 54–55, 60–61, 66–67, 72–73, 76–77, 80–81, 82–83, 88–89, 94–95, 100–101, 104–105, 109, 110–111, 114, 116–117, 122–123, 128–129, 134–135, 140–141, 144–145.

Details of the photographs in the book are as follows:

10–11 Corfe, Dorset; 38 Goldhill, Shaftesbury, Dorset; 44 Virginia creeper, Dorset; 50 Portland lighthouse, Dorset; 59 Rampisham; 62 Fritillaria meleagris; 89 Dianthus 'Ipswich Crimson'; 90 Northam Burrows, Devon; 108 Apeldoorn (Darwin Hybrid) tulip; 118 Rampisham; 136 Durdledoor, Dorset; 146 Frampton-on-Severn.

The publishers would like to thank the following people and organizations for their help in the preparation of this book:

Gamba; Roser Marcé; Jigsaw; The Hat Shop; Whistles; Next B&G; Pineapple Clothing Company; Elizabeth Stuart Smith Shoes; Paul Costelloe; Hilary Bockham; Hyper Hyper; Shelley's Shoes; Twinset; Fenn Wright & Manson; Johnny Moke Shoes; Ben de Lisi; Marina Spadafora; Boyd & Storey.
The bowls photographed on pages 20–21 were made by Joanna Still.
Styling Jody Day; Hair and Make-up Helen Jeffers, Maggie Hunt; Models Laura O'Toole (Select), Amanda King (Zed), Maxine Restall (Models 1), Brenda Edwards, child models from Rascals.

Project Editor    Cortina Butler
Art Editor    Karen Bowen
Copy Editor    Michelle Clark
Picture Research    Nadine Bazar
Production    Jackie Kernaghan
Editorial Assistant    Denise Bates
Special Photography    Anthony Crickmay, Jan Baldwin
Knitting Consultant    Maureen Briggs
Knitting Charts    Radius